Finding more

REAL-LIFE STORIES
WORTH TELLING

Finding More
Copyright © Christianity Explored Ministries 2019
www.christianityexplored.org

Published by:
The Good Book Company

Tel (US): 866 244 2165
Tel (UK): 0333 123 0880
Email (US): info@thegoodbook.com
Email (UK): info@thegoodbook.co.uk

Websites:
North America: www.thegoodbook.com
UK: www.thegoodbook.co.uk
Australia: www.thegoodbook.com.au
New Zealand: www.thegoodbook.co.nz

ISBN: 9781784983673 | Printed in the UK

Design by André Parker

Contents

Introduction

by Rico Tice

If someone asked you to tell your life story in twelve minutes, what would you say?

What would you include? What would you make sure you left out? Which pivotal moments and life-defining relationships would you need to cover?

In mine, I'd include my birth (it was a fairly fundamental moment, though I have no recollection of it), by caesarean section along with my twin sister. I'd talk about discovering that I was dyslexic, and the way I struggled with that all through my school days… I'd mention playing loads of sports as a teenager (no one asks you to spell on a hockey pitch). I'd describe my first job, as a youthworker in inner-city Liverpool, and how that shaped me. And I'd include getting married and having three kids.

I might leave out the time I was picked to captain the West of England cricket team for my age group. It was a huge honour, and I turned up that Saturday, excited and proud, to discover that the match had been on the Friday.

I would skip over the time, not long after I became a church pastor, that I was summoned to court and banned from driving for six months because I kept speeding and I got caught. My wife still has the newspaper cutting stuck to a cupboard in our kitchen.

Every life story is different—with different hopes, views, regrets, achievements. So what would be in yours?

Well, the eleven people you're about to meet really did sit down with someone and tell their life story. Each of them was interviewed by a friend of mine, Rachel Jones. These are their twelve minutes, written down. Each of them have left in some parts they might rather have left out. They're all very different from each other—with different backgrounds, nationalities, colours, careers, experiences, personalities and difficulties. But, as you'll see, all of them found something more, right in the midst of the ups and downs and ordinary days and special days that make up life as a human being. Thanks for taking the time to listen to them.

I think you'll find them fascinating, because—well—people are fascinating. And I think you'll find them helpful too. After all, your story is as yet unfinished. And perhaps an even more fascinating question than "What would you include in your life story so far?" is "What would you like to be included in the next few chapters of your life?"

Most of us, however we got to where we are right now, are hoping for something different, something new, something more in life. A new relationship, or experience, or promotion, or location. Maybe you're reading this and your life story has taken a few wrong turns, and you'd love to work out how to get yourself heading in the right direction. Maybe you're reading this and you've always kept things on track, and yet the track never quite seems to get you to where you'd hoped to be and how you'd hoped you'd feel. Maybe you're feeling content right now—but still every now and then you wonder whether there might be something more.

This book is an opportunity to look at life through a different pair of eyes—an invitation to enjoy the stories of these people's lives, and perhaps to find inspiration and direction as you chart your own.

"I knew I still hadn't found it"

Katie's story

Katie looks how most people feel at 9 p.m. on a weeknight after work: tired. She's changed into a stripy red and white top, taken off her make-up and pulled her dark hair back into a ponytail.

She's Skyping from her flat in Shenzhen, China. It's monsoon season—hot and humid. As she speaks, the draught from the air conditioning keeps blowing her hair into her face. She pushes it back with a sweep of her hand, saying, "Recently I have been so busy with… life".

For most of her 20s, Katie's "life" = work.

"I just wanted to be considered a success," she says, looking back. "That was my goal. In the company I worked for, your whole team would get ranked at the end of the year, from the best performer down to the worst. No one wanted to be the loser. So every year I had a performance target in mind, and I worked really hard to achieve it so I wouldn't get pushed down the rankings. I would get into the office and be so focused on work that the next thing I knew it was already three or four o'clock in the afternoon. A ten-hour day was a good day, but sometimes it was twelve."

Where did her drive come from? "I think from my parents— especially my mother, because she had her own business. For her, your wealth was your worth. I guess she grew up in a time in China's history when everyone was very poor, so she was proud of the fact that she had made a name for herself."

Katie was born in what would be considered a "small town" by Chinese standards, but a city by any other. Like almost everyone else in her generation, she was an only child. Her parents were atheists, "but even though they didn't believe in God, they still tried to raise me with a value system and a sense of right and wrong. But I was not the kind of kid who just did what their parents told them. I was very strong-minded, strong-willed—an independent thinker. As I grew into a teenager, those differences of opinion led to some... heated conversations."

And it was a major argument with her mother when she was 15 that made Katie determined to study abroad. "I just wanted to be as far away as possible. And I succeeded—I left China at the age of 18 to come to university in the UK."

She got a job in the UK after graduating, and a decade later, her determination had paid off again with more success. "Outwardly, I had what everybody else would have called a very successful career. I earned a lot more than my peers. I could afford to travel; I was going on four international trips a year. I lived in a nice area of the city. I was hanging out with important people. I should have been content. But really, I felt empty inside."

Katie couldn't shake the gnawing sense that none of it really mattered. "I started thinking about the bigger questions of life: 'Why am I here? What is the meaning of living a life?' At first, it was just occasional thoughts. I would push them into the corner of my mind and just think about something else. But gradually they became more and more of a concern. I would be on my way to work, thinking, 'Katie, you know this is not fulfilling you, so why are you still doing this? What's the point of all this anyway?'"

Eventually, Katie knew she needed to find some answers: "So, like many modern people, I went to a therapist. I had sessions for about nine or ten months. I went through my childhood issues, and that was really healthy for me. But it didn't go anywhere. It still didn't answer the questions of why I was born into this world, or what the meaning of life is.

"So then I moved on to philosophy. I enrolled myself on courses. I even went to a summer school at a university. But I started to realise that philosophy is a subject that's not about answers but questions. There aren't any proper answers—they use one question to answer another question. That's what philosophy was to me, at least," she says with a self-deprecating smile. "So I decided, 'Okay, this is not gonna help me either. I need something else.'"

Next up was religion: "As I am Chinese, Buddhism is kind of the go-to, default religion. So I travelled to several monasteries in the UK to talk to the monks and try to get a sense of meaning. I studied the Buddhist scriptures. I learned to meditate. And although reading the scriptures kind of calmed me, they still didn't have the answer. I knew I still hadn't found it. I didn't know what 'it' was, but I knew I hadn't found it."

Around that time, Katie remembered that one of her friends was a Christian. But she was reluctant to ask her about it: "It's funny—although I was willing to look into Buddhism, I still felt like people who believed in God must be really stupid. I thought they just needed a crutch to lean on. But eventually I decided to speak to this friend. She was living in a different city, so I had to call her. We spent two hours on the phone together. At the beginning of the call, I was speaking like a normal friend would, like, 'Hi, I just wanted to chat about your faith' and all that. But over the duration of the phone call, I realised I had this anger coming out towards her. It really shocked me. I was saying things like, 'If there is a God, why is there so much suffering in the world? Why has he let bad things happen to me? How does this make any sense?' It almost felt like I was venting my anger at God through my friend. And to my surprise, she took it well. Wow—" Katie says, almost laughing in surprise now, "she took it *really* well. She didn't try to rush in answering my questions, but she just really gently engaged me in that conversation. She came across like she had a peace that I just didn't have. That really struck me. I thought, 'OK, if that's what your faith does to you, then I want to find out about it'."

Towards the end of the phone call, Katie's friend suggested she should try going to church. "She told me I should just go and see for myself. I said yes because she had been so kind to me on the phone, and I felt guilty for being so angry. I thought I would leave church after ten minutes—then at least I could tell her that I'd tried."

But when she went to church, Katie didn't leave early. The music was nice; but it was the Bible talk that really hit her. "It was based on a story Jesus told, and something clicked inside me. At the end of the sermon we stood up to sing, and as I was reading the lyrics, something just overcame me—this overwhelming feeling of love. It's hard to describe… For the first time in my life I felt completely safe. Not physically safe, but like, supernaturally safe. I remember I came out of the church building and I was a little bit shocked at myself."

She joined a group at the church where they met to read the Bible and talk about it. "I was so struck by this person called Jesus," she remembers now. "I thought, 'If this is a made-up storybook, then this character is absolutely perfect'. I loved reading books. Books can touch you. But this was something different. I was so drawn to this personality that was just so full of love. Like, Jesus was constantly surrounded by crowds of people. There was this time when he tried to take his closest friends, the twelve disciples, away for a break because they were all so tired. They got in a boat to cross the lake to a quieter place

"For the first time in my life I felt completely safe."

away from the crowds, but when they arrived at the shore, they realised the people had followed them there on foot. It says that 'when Jesus landed and saw a large crowd, he had compassion on them, because they were like sheep without a shepherd' (Mark 6:34). That really struck me, because there have been many times when I've felt so tired that the only thing I want to do is just to escape from people! But Jesus, even though he was really tired, as soon as he saw people's needs, he responded to them."

But as Katie read more and more about Jesus, she came up against a problem: Jesus made some big claims about himself. "This really loving person, who I felt so drawn to, also said he was the Son of God—God himself, walking on earth as a human. He said that he was the 'Christ', the 'Messiah'—the

King that God had promised to send hundreds of years before. I knew I kind of had to make a decision—was he telling the truth or not? I realised that if this person Jesus was true, he was the best person I would ever come across in my whole life. But if he said he was the Son of God and was lying, then he wasn't such a good-hearted, loving person after all. That would be a contradiction. But as I read about his character and the loving things he did, eventually I became convinced that he really must be who he said he was: the Son of God. I could trust him."

Now, as she looks back on her search for answers, Katie wishes she'd started, as well as finished, her search with Jesus: "He's the One that every person is looking for. Everyone has something that you think is so important that you need to treasure it. For most of my twenties, that was my work. Perhaps for some other people that could be a boyfriend or girlfriend, or their parents'

"I knew I had to make a decision – was Jesus telling the truth or not?"

or friends' approval. But living for these things will take all the energy we have. Whatever we do, we'll still feel like we are not enough. Even in the best human relationships, there's an element of transaction there—I'll do this for you, because you do this for me. But in Jesus, I have found someone who will always love me more than I love him. I don't think we can find that kind of love from any human being. It's only God who can give unconditionally without any strings attached. So when we ask him to fill our needs, he can."

A few years after becoming a Christian, Katie met up with a colleague who she hadn't worked with for a while. "She said to me, 'Katie, at first we thought you were crazy with all this Christian stuff. But now every time I see you, you just become happier and happier. There's almost a glow on your face, and it's not just a front that you're trying to put on. Maybe there is something to Jesus.'"

So why is Katie so happy? Because, she says, she's found the answer to that question which plagued her for so long: what is the point of life?

"Now I live my life for Christ. It's like, if someone has given you 10 million in the bank, you probably wouldn't think much of giving a handful of change to someone on the street. Jesus has given me so much love that now I'm trying to share that love that I have received from him with the people around me. That's when you live your life to the fullest. I can honestly say that the more I grow in my faith, the more alive I feel."

"I wanted the evidence"

Larry's story

L arry is an actuary. He describes it as being "a super accountant: like an accountant, but with even more maths".

Today he's working from home. "Home" for Larry has that sense of relaxed chaos which comes with having three children aged 4-10. They're at school this morning, but there's plenty of evidence of them in the busy kitchen-diner.

Larry makes coffee while clearing a space at the end of the dining table, stacking up superhero comics, notebooks and bank statements at one end of it. There's a fish tank in the corner that's probably due its next clean, and near it a table-football table—one of Larry's prized possessions. It turns out that not all the toys are for the kids. "My wife bought it for me for my birthday a few years back. I think she's regretted it ever since. It takes up far too much space, but I love it. It's so much fun."

If Larry's down-to-earth kitchen isn't what you might expect of a "super-accountant", his background conforms a little more to type. His parents were very driven and put a big emphasis on studying hard and performing well at school. They wanted to see Larry and his sister grow up to be successful. They were first-generation immigrants who emigrated from Mauritius—a little island off the east coast of Africa.

Larry admits that despite his parents' best efforts, he was a somewhat lazy student. But you get the impression that he was a clever one too.

His family were Catholics, so Larry went to mass regularly as a child and even served as an altar boy for a time. But what didn't make sense to him about religion when he was growing up was the maths. Going to confession sticks in his mind as a slightly scary experience: "You needed to think of a sin to confess to the priest. It needed to be bad enough to show the priest that you had taken it seriously. But not so bad that you didn't mind telling it to this man on the other side of a screen in a little box."

After you had confessed your sin, the priest would set you "penance"—a set number of prayers you had to say to make up for your wrongdoing. And this was where the maths was a problem: "Sometimes you would confess a big sin and get away with only having to say one prayer as penance. Other times you would confess to something small—like breaking a couple of promises—and you'd get stung with five. It seemed random. The numbers didn't add up."

By the time Larry went to university (to study economics, naturally), he'd given up on church completely. But when, in his final year, he discovered that a girl he liked went to church, he saw it as his opportunity to impress. "I remember thinking, 'Church? I can do church.' So I started going along."

What he found, though, was something very different to the type of church he'd been used to as a kid. The biggest difference was in the preaching—much to his surprise, he actually enjoyed it. "The guy at the front was talking about the Bible, and somehow it just seemed really practical and relevant to real life. At the church I grew up going to, you went along just hoping the sermon wasn't going to go on too long. But at this church the preacher spoke like it was true and it really mattered."

Something about it had Larry hooked. So he went along, on and off, even when things with the girl fizzled out. And when he moved city at the end of university, he found a new church to

"I realised that the stakes were pretty high. If Christianity was true, it mattered."

go to. "I realised that the stakes were pretty high. If Christianity was true, it mattered. So I couldn't just walk away—I kept coming back."

But at the same time, he didn't want to get too sucked into "all that Christian stuff". Larry remembers being curious but uncomfortable. He tended to make a quick exit at the end of the last hymn and avoided speaking to anyone. During the week, he worked hard; at the weekend, he played hard. Other than his peculiar church-going habit, Larry's life looked much like any other young city professional's.

Larry tells me about a colleague at work with whom he's recently been having conversations about Christianity. Like many people, she wants the evidence. Larry sympathises. "I wanted the evidence too. But the thing you've got to ask yourself is, what kind of evidence will be enough? What is the evidence that you're looking for? I get that the miracles in the Bible sound outrageous—the story with Jesus multiplying a few loaves of bread and fish to feed a whole crowd, for example. But I can't dismiss that just because I've not seen it happen in my lifetime. That's not evidence that it can't happen. If God created the world, then why not?"

So what evidence turned out to be enough for Larry? "It comes down to two things," he explains. "The first is the physical evidence—the Bible.

"I had dismissed it as a collection of stories for children, or a fake cooked up by some nutters trying to start their own religion. But that can't really be true. The four Gospels, for example, are short biographies about the life, death and—

"Why would they die for something they knew to be a lie?"

most controversially—alleged resurrection of Jesus. These were written using eyewitness testimony, within living memory of Jesus' time on earth in the first century.

"As with any ancient document, none of the originals survive today. What we have is copies of the originals (or more rightly, copies of copies of copies, and so on). What marks the Gospels out from other documents from ancient history, like the writings of Julius Caesar or Homer, is the number of copies available. This means that they can be compared for accuracy.

"The key events of Jesus' life are attested to in the writings of various ancient historians who weren't Christians. Jesus was a real historical figure who lived in Israel in the first century. That much isn't up for debate.

"But it was what happened to the first generation of Christians that convinced me. They claimed to have seen Jesus be killed and then come back to life again." He points out that many of them were put to death for saying that.

Sure, but lots of people die for what they believe in, right? Today you hear of suicide bombers who have been brainwashed in the name of religion.

Larry shakes his head. "This was different. It's one thing to willingly die because you've been promised some kind of reward. But those Christians were being killed for stating they'd seen Jesus alive—it wasn't something they believed but something they'd seen. Why would they die for something they knew to be a lie?"

After going to church for a couple of years, Larry eventually decided to take the plunge and go on a course that the church was running, called *Christianity Explored*. It was designed for people who wanted to investigate Christianity for themselves. He says he doesn't remember much about the first few weeks in that crowded room in the church's basement, other than the fact that he enjoyed them. But as the course went on, Larry says, he realised that what Jesus said about what people are like and what people need rang true. Jesus talked about "sin" not as things people do but as an attitude they have deep inside—an attitude that Larry recognised in his own heart for the first time. That was the second piece of evidence—that the Bible matches up with the reality of life. "I realised I needed a relationship with God. Instead of trying to think up trivial sins to confess to the priest, I needed to genuinely ask Jesus to forgive me."

So did life change after that? "Oh, probably not enough," he admits, wiping his glasses on the edge of his t-shirt. Change did come... but very gradually. That's the thing about faith, apparently. You don't necessarily have a fizz-bang moment and "become a Christian". More often you just slowly find that yes—the evidence stacks up, yes—what Jesus says about you is true, and yes—you want the kind of friendship with God that the Bible talks about.

Aside from the table football, Larry's other favourite item in the room is the big range cooker in the kitchen. "I love eating, and so I love cooking," he smiles. One of his projects at the moment is trying to perfect his mother's recipes and record them before her memory goes. She was diagnosed with dementia a few years ago. At the moment the family are trying to support her in being as independent as she can be for as long as she can be. At the back of the garden—past the swing set and the barbecue that are ready and waiting for summer—is a little bungalow, ready and waiting for her to move into when the time comes. "We're very lucky to have been able to buy it," Larry says. "It came onto the market three weeks after my dad died. We were all worried about mum being left on her own, and he had left us a bit of money, so that's what we spent it on."

When, a little earlier in the interview, Larry is asked what significant moments he's had in the years since he became a Christian, it's his father's death that he chooses. It was quite sudden—he had a stroke caused by a brain haemorrhage. "For most of his life, if you'd have asked my dad what was most important to him, he would have said it was to have his family around him on his deathbed, knowing that they were well provided for. And there we were, gathered round him while he lay there unconscious in a hospital bed. My sister and I both had successful jobs like Dad wanted.

"But it struck me that even though he had all the things he would have said were most important to him, none of it really mattered. He was dying. The only thing that actually mattered then was whether God exists, and whether Dad had a relationship with him that would see him through the other side of death.

"My experience of watching Dad die made me realise how important the issue of looking into God is," Larry reflects now. "So many of my friends aren't opposed to Christianity or religion per se; they just choose not to engage with it in any shape or form. But what I want to say is, *Please don't go through life not looking into the evidence.* You'd never pitch up at an important job interview without preparing for it—you'd prepare by reading about the company, the job you're going for, and the background of the people who are going to be interviewing you. So why would you treat your own death less seriously than a job interview?"

Larry says that facing up to the inevitability of death in the future makes a huge difference to life in the present too. "Life is full of stresses and things that go wrong. And if this is all there is, then that's a real problem. But Jesus promises that his people will have life on the other side of death—that's fantastic. And it's not just for the future. A relationship with God helps you to enjoy life now more too." Even more than super-accountancy, it seems—and even more than table football.

"The religious people I knew were hypocrites"

Caroline's story

C aroline boarded a plane to London to find herself—but she ended up finding something very different.

Today, 17 years later, she's Skyping in for this interview from a suburb of Dublin, Ireland, where she lives now with her husband, Jeff, and four kids. "Irish people are just so likeable," she says, with a still-noticeable American accent. "There's really no other place I'd rather be."

It's just as well—her now-husband told her on their first date that he was always going to move back to Ireland. They met in London, when Caroline was moving in to start a new job at a place where Jeff had just finished working. "We already knew of each other through mutual friends. He was coming to get his final box of stuff to take it up to his new place, just as I was moving in. Then he drove past me on the road and pulled over and said, 'Do you want a ride?' I was on my way to get my belongings out of storage, and before I knew it, he'd spent all day moving my stuff."

Four years later she moved with him to Dublin as his wife.

Caroline's accent is hard to place any more precisely than as "American". She started life in Virginia, but then moved several times around various states, mainly in the south-east, until she graduated from college (and a different one from where she started). "I was probably quite a people-pleaser as a teenager," she says. "I wanted to do well at school, although I was never at the top of my class. I was involved in lots of sports and kept really busy. I just wanted to seem OK to everybody else."

Caroline grew up going to church but didn't always like what she found there. "So many of the religious people I knew were hypocrites. I knew some genuine, loving Christians—friends' parents who really took me into their lives and cared for me like their own daughter. But I also knew lots of people whose faith didn't seem to affect them outside of Sunday services. They said one thing in public but in private did another. In reality they were the complete opposite of what you would want to be as a person. The way people spoke in church made it sound like becoming a Christian made all your problems go away, but I knew that was a lie. So I began to be weighed down by the idea that I didn't know what was really true, or how to know what that was. Faith seemed like this mystical thing that some people had and some people didn't—and lots of people were just faking. I was so confused about who God was."

Caroline's view of God was also affected by difficult circumstances at home. Caroline is very guarded about that time in her life, because she wants to protect her family and has resolved never to criticise them publicly. But by the time she was about to graduate from college, the issues that had marked her childhood were coming to a head, and made God seem even further away: "It felt like everything in my whole life had fallen apart. I didn't feel like I had anything left. And I just thought, 'What are you doing, God? How am I supposed to see you or understand you? How can you be good when you're taking everything away?' I felt let down and desperate."

It was at her lowest point that Caroline moved to London, desperate to get away and leave her past behind her. In her first few months there, she "came alive"—and she almost seems to come alive as she talks about it now. "I met someone on the plane who was also in the same situation as me—another let's-move-to-London-and-see-how-life-works-out type of person—and we helped each other find hostels when we arrived. I loved the city right from the beginning. There's so much going on. I found a good job in PR that I enjoyed, and I had the nicest boss in the whole world. She was just lovely. And I was so excited to be financially independent for the first time in my life; I got a real sense of satisfaction from earning a paycheque and looking after myself."

But what Caroline was most excited about finding was a church. And not just any church. She had been to a particular London church while she had been backpacking around Europe a few years before. She wanted to go back, but she couldn't remember what it was called or how to find it. "It was like looking for a needle in a haystack."

A friend from the US put her in touch with a friend of hers in London, who invited Caroline to a church. "That first Sunday morning I walked in and slowly realised that it was that *exact* church I had been looking for. I remember sitting down and looking up at the yellow walls and the big marble columns and the balcony and thinking, 'Yeah, this is it'. As we were singing the first hymn, the emotion of it all overwhelmed me. I sat on the pew and cried all the way through. It felt like God had been so kind to me by putting this girl on the plane next to me when I was going alone over to a new place, and in giving me the job. So I had this deep sense already that God was there with me, protecting me and helping me... And then finally landing in this church that I wanted to find but didn't even know where to begin the search for. I didn't think anyone but God could have planned for me to end up there again."

Her voice cracks and her eyes well up as she remembers the emotions of that moment. "It was like God was beginning to answer those questions I had of 'Are you good? Do you care? Have you given up on me?' He was working in such a significant way to show me tender love and care, which I clearly didn't deserve. So I was sitting there, crying and crying, and the girl sitting next to me offered me a tissue. It turned out that she became my very good friend."

From that moment on, Caroline was like a sponge—she went to everything she could that the church was running, including a course for people who wanted to investigate Christianity for the first time or just brush up on their knowledge of the Bible.

This proved to be particularly significant. "At the first session, the minister who was running it stood up and said, 'Many of you here have been hurt or let down by the church, or by Christian people, in the past. So can I say as a minister, on behalf of the church in general, that I'm so sorry that happened. But please, on this course try to put that to one side and just look—*really* look—at the person of Jesus Christ. Read about him in the Bible, see who he is, and decide what you make of him. Because that's what Christianity is all about—Jesus.' That may sound like the most obvious thing in the world, but it was a very helpful thing for me to hear in that moment because I was still wounded by the Christian hypocrisy I had seen growing up."

And so Caroline took up the invitation to "look" at Jesus.

"I was struck by the way that Jesus was so strong and bold and unafraid. He was so certain of who he was. In Jesus' time there were these religious types, called the Pharisees. They put on a big show of having it all together—they were kind of like the religious hypocrites that I had encountered in my own life. And I discovered that Jesus didn't like those Pharisees either. He was always confronting them. He wasn't afraid; he was really strong. But at the same time... the way that he treated *anyone* who came to him feeling broken and messed up inside was so gentle and so loving."

She retells the story of a time when Jesus was at a dinner party, hosted by one of these Pharisees. "A woman with a bad reputation came in—the kind of woman whose past made her a social outcast. She was crying and crying, and she wet Jesus' feet with her tears, dried them with her hair, kissed them and poured perfume on them. The Pharisee whose party it was was immediately judgmental: 'If this man [Jesus] were a prophet, he

"Jesus didn't care what people would think."

would know who is touching him and what kind of woman she is' (Luke 7:39). But Jesus didn't care what people would think. Instead, in front of everyone there, he called out the Pharisee for being a terrible, rude host. Then he commended the woman for showing him genuine love. So Jesus didn't shun the woman like everyone else did—he spoke up for her. Time and again you see the same thing in the Bible. Broken people felt able to approach Jesus, but the religious people who didn't think they needed any help were repelled by him."

Something about those stories resonated deeply with Caroline. "I was very much feeling like a broken person at that time too. I would still lose sleep at night over things that I had done in my past. No one else knew about them because I was trying to maintain that perfect package on the outside. But there were these tarnishes inside me that I knew about. And when I saw the way Jesus interacted with people who felt like that, he became so appealing to me. I just *loved* him."

After she had been going along to the course for a while, Caroline realised that, like the woman in the story, she wanted a clean slate from Jesus too. "In the books we were using for the course, there was this prayer that you could use to commit your life to following Jesus. It had a line that was something like, 'Please take complete control of my life'. I had said that kind of prayer dozens of times before when I had been growing up. So I left that session early, to give other people space to think and talk about it. But I went home, and I couldn't sleep with the burden of the fact that I had never really given my heart to Christ—not like this. Not in a way that would mean that he would be in charge. I wanted to have control of my own life, not give it to someone else. Yet the words of Jesus kept pounding in my heart. I could see that there was no way to take these things that I was learning about him and leave them on the sidelines. I didn't sleep at all that night. So the next morning I really gave my life to him. I knew that Jesus was someone I could trust my life with."

And that was a turning point. "Everything seemed different. I mean, the world was the same, but my priorities had changed." Gradually, she saw that she needed to reach out to the family she had cut herself off from and repair those relationships. As she speaks about them now, she is very careful to protect them—a change that she says is testament to the difference her faith has made to her.

Looking at Caroline now, it's hard to imagine her as the messy young woman she says she once was. She is confident, articulate and attractive. Life with four kids is full but happy, her days taken up with walks in the sunshine, trips to Dublin Zoo, reading books to the kids after dinner, and family film nights watching *Star Wars* movies. It's the kind of steady, contented family life that her younger self must have never thought possible.

But sometimes, she says, it helps her to remember who she is inside really. "I was thinking about this before this interview, while I was feeding my baby daughter her bottle. What is it from my journey that still sticks with me? It's 17 years on, and I'm married and I'm a mother and I'm a member of our church here, and sometimes I can pretend that I'm all good really. That I'm better now. And I start to feel a bit like the Pharisee—like I'm neat and tidy and don't really need Jesus' help. But that attitude never goes well. Even now, I'm still learning that I still have to come to Jesus each day, bringing him my mess and my weakness and my worries, and asking him for help. It's when I come to him like that that my relationship with him is so sweet."

"I thought Christianity was a white man's religion"

Jason's story

Jason remembers the day his foster mother told him he'd end up in prison: "She looked at me at the dinner table and she said, 'Jay, you're going to get weighed off one day'."
Jason pauses, and looks at me across the marble-topped table of the coffee-shop booth: "You know what 'weighed off' means, yeah? Like, weighed off to prison." He laughs at my ignorance—a loud cackle that's hard not to laugh along with.

The conversation continues much like this. Jason's story is a blur of names and events. There's a sad sort of inevitability to the start of it: "When I was about a year old, me and my twin brother, Kevin, was found in a flat. The landlord heard two babies crying, kicked the door open and there we was. We went straight into care. At school I was always fighting and getting into trouble. I got suspended three times—one of them was for burning down the science lab. They called my mum up to the school once, and my head teacher said, 'Jason needs to see a psychiatrist for his behaviour'. My mum pushed back and said, 'He don't need to see a psychiatrist. He's just a naughty kid.' But that's the same story for lots of black kids now," he says, shaking his head. "So many black boys are still free-falling through the education system." Jay was one of them, leaving school with only one qualification, a D-grade in pottery.

Outside of school, Jay used to fight with skinheads who belonged to the National Front, the white-supremacist political party. But this was the 1980s, and soon a type of racial unity emerged from an unlikely source: the acid rave scene. "All

"I thought, 'If there's a God, you owe me one. All I am is a good, honest drug dealer.'"

of a sudden black and white come together, raving. It broke down barriers. We used to drive to these raves with probably about 65,000 people in a field, dancing. Clubbers, Hip Hop Heads, breakdance enthusiasts, graffiti artists—people from an array of backgrounds. Everyone seemed to be at these raves. And I remember someone walking past me at this rave with two buckets: a bucket of ecstasy pills and a bucket of puff [cannabis]. He was walking through this crowd going, 'Pills, puff, pills, puff, pills, puff'—people was just buying drugs out of buckets! And I remember looking at them buckets and I thought to myself, 'There's money to be made there'. So I went from partygoer to party drug dealer."

Jay spent the next few years like this—raving and drug dealing. Until it all went wrong: "I was in a club with £800 in one pocket, 42 ecstasy pills in the other pocket. We was all about to go home after a really good night. And I felt two hands on my hands, pinning them in my pocket. Two bouncers." Jay was arrested and spent the night in a police cell. "When I got arrested that night, a friend of mine who'd gone out and left the club early realised that I hadn't come out of the club. He phoned my girlfriend, and he said, 'Julie, do me a favour. Jay's been nicked—get to the flat and clear it out.' Julie went to the flat, cleared out all the coke and everything, and as she walked out of the building with a big bag with all my drugs in it, the police walked past her on their way to raid my flat. There was nothing in there."

But that wasn't enough to save Jay from a prison sentence—and neither was the dodgy solicitor he hired to get him off the hook. "The person I got the drugs from, he said to me once, 'Always remember, if you play the game, you've got to be willing to pay the game'." The payment was four years in jail.

To Jason, that didn't feel fair: "I remember being sat on my bed in my cell one day, and I was really angry. I said, 'If there's a God out there—if you're real—you absolutely owe me. All I am is a good, honest drug dealer. And you've put me in prison.'" What, no moral pangs at all? "I said, 'Listen, Lord. I ain't broken into no one's house. I ain't killed no one. I'm polite.' Even though we were selling drugs, we had a code of conduct. We respected women; we respected the elderly. We never, ever went looking for trouble, but we handled it if it came our way. We just used to enjoy ourselves. And then God had me put inside."

When Jason came out of jail, he went back to the drugs trade—but on a scale that made his party drug dealing look like small fry. He started working for a man who was, in his own words, "a villain—hardcore". He explains, with his voice lowered, "I got involved in importation. Bringing over keys and keys and keys [kilos] of drugs across from Europe. Landing it on the beach, loading it in a van, and then going all over the city." Jay catches himself whispering and laughs. "I don't know why I'm whispering! It's funny, you get into it—like it's back in the day and I'm gonna get weighed off again."

The fact that Jay can laugh about it now shows how much has changed in the last 18 years. He looks right at home in this sleek coffee shop, drinking a flat white and working on his Macbook like any other law-abiding citizen. When he takes off his green-knit jumper, it's clear he's in good shape—it's only the flecks of grey in his beard which suggest he's closer to fifty than forty.

But his words paint a picture of a younger man whose life was slowly unravelling: "By this time I was doing loads of coke. I was selling six keys of coke in the morning and then doing it myself at 11 a.m. I was living with my girl—had two children. Julie said, 'Jay, you're addicted to cocaine now'. And I probably was. I was doing it all the time." He recalls an incident when some drugs went missing. He had to go to a meeting with his boss's bosses, not knowing whether he was going to make it back alive. They could have killed him and disposed of the evidence without a trace.

Even though Jay was "making a bundle of cash", he ended up putting himself in debt. In fact, this is the one point in the interview when Jay asks the recording to be stopped, as he reveals quite how much money he managed to blow in the space of nine months. It was a lot.

It was in this time of chaos that Julie started going to church: "She come back one afternoon and she'd heard about this person called Jesus Christ. I went absolutely mad, I did, because in my eyes Christianity was a slave religion. It was a white man's religion." Jay tries to explain what this means: "Growing up in care, getting into trouble at school, all that, I was… we were trying to work out who we were. Our Bible then was a book by Chancellor Williams called *The Destruction of Black Civilization*," he says, bringing up the

"I smashed up the house to get her to stop. But she kept going to church."

cover on his laptop. "It wasn't just a book to me; it was my identity. Growing up in care I was really angry, thinking, 'It shouldn't be like this, not knowing my real mum'. I knew so many other black kids in broken families, broken homes. And this book explained who I was, where I came from, and that all this is the legacy of the slave trade. Slave masters always used to break up families; it stopped rebellion." In the words of the tattoo which his twin brother Kev had inked into his leg, Jay was "black and proud".

Which was why his girlfriend's interest in Christianity was a problem: "I didn't need her bringing home some white dead dude on a cross. I said to her, 'Do me a favour; don't teach that to my son'. But she kept going to church. So I tried to intimidate her to get her to stop. I smashed up my house. I mean, *I smashed it up*. Tore all the doors off the kitchen cupboards. Kicked the door down. Smashed all the plates. Kicked the bannisters out. Ruined downstairs. Decimated it. I was drinking, taking cocaine—I just went wild. But she kept on going to church.

"One day there was a knock on the door and a pastor come in my front room. I'd just made £6,000 that day. So I'm like, on top of the world. I'm in my front room watching TV, and in comes this white older pastor, and he's trying to tell me about Jesus Christ. And I think, 'I ain't gonna put up with this'. I said to him, 'OK, do me a favour, fella. You're either gonna leave my house now, or I'm gonna roll you up and post you through my letterbox to get you out of my house.' And my girlfriend was sat on the stairs, listening and praying. But this pastor carried on going on about Jesus. I thought to myself, 'This bloke's either really, really stupid, or he must be good at fighting'."

Eventually the pastor left. But Julie's interest in Christianity continued to grow. "I come back one morning from being out doing coke all night. I was a hot-blooded man, looking forward to seeing my girlfriend. She turned round and said to me, 'I can't have a physical relationship with you again. I'm following Jesus now, and we're not married, and I don't think it's right. I can't have sex with you again.' Honestly, I nearly fell off my chair. I was like, you've got to be joking. You've *got to be joking*. This is going well overboard. I can't believe this."

Things continued to get worse—or better, depending on which way you look at it. "One evening, loads of Christians come round my house and we were all squashed in the front room. They got these Bibles out, and was looking at a part of the Bible called Romans. We read this bit where it says, 'For all have sinned and fall short of the glory of God' (Romans 3:23). And I read that, and it was like it was speaking about my life."

When he was in prison, Jay had felt like he'd done nothing wrong against God. But now it was different. "I knew; I just knew that my life was wrong. I knew it wasn't right. I knew that bit of the Bible was speaking about me, really—I had sinned.

And a bit later Romans says this: 'The wages of sin is death, but the gift of God is eternal life in Christ Jesus our Lord' (Romans 6:23). I was so deep in the drugs trade… people went 'missing' all the time. I could have been next to go. But I knew then that I deserved more than death from God for my sin."

This was a revelation for Jay. He laughs as he remembers speaking to his friends: "I said, 'Boys, I have just read the Bible, and I have never ever known anything like it. It was like it was alive.' I realised this wasn't just for white people. I couldn't put my finger on how, but the Bible just… spoke about my life. It was so wise; it so made sense."

Now Jay was torn—torn between his old life and one with Jesus in it: "Sometimes if my girlfriend wasn't there when the Christians came for Bible study, I used to hear their car

"When the Christians came for Bible study I'd turn the lights off and pretend I wasn't in."

doors slam, and then I'd turn the lights off, lock the door, and pretend I wasn't in," he laughs. Why? "Because I wanted to get on with my life. I knew that becoming a Christian was a choice; it was a sacrifice. You've got to give it all up. From my background, it's a massive decision. But I knew God was calling me. I remember getting on my knees once, praying to God that I wanted to be a Christian. And I had a long list on my wall, stuck up in the kitchen, of all the things I was going to stop: *stop dealing, stop doing drugs, stop doing this, stop doing that.* But I kept doing all those things. I was still going out—

I'd go on the Friday night and come back Sunday morning. If I went to church with Julie, she would always give me some mints because I smelt of alcohol.

"I come home one morning after I'd been out and I remember looking at Julie… and I could see the disappointment in her eyes. I said to her, 'What do you expect of me? I'm Jay Marriner. The culture of the street, dealing and everything—it's ingrained in me. It's who I am. I'm not like all those other Christians—those Christians who have grown up in Christian homes and they're really nice. It ain't my bag. I can't do it.'

"And I remember all of a sudden sitting in my front room, and I broke down in tears. And I heard God say to me—not audibly, I don't know how but I heard him say—'Guess what, you muppet, *you can't do it.* That's the point. Because Christ has already done it.' Then the penny dropped. I realised God was saying you can't do it by a list. I needed to give up trying to be good enough on my own and ask him to help me. I needed him to forgive me, and I needed him to change me."

And in the two decades since, he has. If you need proof that Jesus can change anyone, from any background, it's Jay Marriner. Now he is Julie's husband, a father of seven, and a pastor—he's in this coffee shop working on his Bible talk for Sunday. He set up, or "planted", the church he leads five years ago. Explaining why, he says, "I've seen Jesus radically transform my life—so I know he can do that for anyone. He isn't just for one kind of person, or one kind of background. He's for everyone. And in my community, we need him. I come from a community who are absolutely decimated. Young people who've been through the criminal justice system. Some around here are also involved in gangs. Gun and knife crime happens. The local housing estates breed crime, and there is poverty. Some regeneration has happened, but some things stay the same. I am aware that about 90% of the people in my church have never even grown up with a dad in their life. There are good things going on too, but at the same time there are so many needs, so many broken lives. The only person who can offer any real hope is the only person who could offer me hope—Jesus."

"I got up and started shouting abuse at the speaker"

Drew's story

"I've always been the sort of person who when I do something, I do it properly—I go all in," says Drew. For the first twenty years of his life, the obsession was music.

"I basically fell in love with music at about the age of ten, and set my mind on being a professional musician. Pretty soon life revolved around that. Every night after school I'd usually do three different things—piano lesson, followed by choir practice, followed by orchestra, and so on. There was always something. Even as a kid I would be up at 5:30 in the morning to practise the violin. I'm pretty sure my brothers didn't like that!"

What was it about music that so captured him? "I remember seeing a string quartet playing, and thinking, 'That is amazing. That is what I want to do.' Maybe it was something about the beauty of the sound, or the beauty of the teamwork that goes into performing together as a group. Or maybe just the fact that playing music is *fun*. It's interesting that the word we use is 'play'—you play music; you don't work music. I knew I wanted to spend the rest of my life working by playing."

When Drew was 18, he started at a prestigious "conservatoire" or music college. It was here that Drew took his passion to a whole new level: "If I was obsessive as a kid, I became completely ruthless as a student. Everything was about becoming the best musician I could possibly be. I even used to dump girlfriends if they got in the way of my practice. I gave up drinking alcohol. I would still go out with my friends every night, but because I didn't drink, I could still get up at 5 a.m. the next day to go for a run, eat a huge bowl of cereal and be in the practice room by 7 a.m. I used to practise my scales from 7 a.m. until 10 a.m. every morning without fail. It was nuts…" he says, shaking his head. "It did make me a good musician, though."

Over his four years at university, Drew's determination paid off. "By the age of 21 I was basically living my dream life. I won the competitions I wanted to win. I got into the string quartet I wanted to get into. I was playing solo tours and travelling the world. I'd made it as a musician."

Drew doesn't seem that intense on first meeting. Instead he has an almost boyish charm about him. He's expressive and eager to please—offering up a choice of mugs for coffee and his grandmother's homemade shortbread—with sandy blond hair, a clean-shaven jawline and round glasses. It's a warm day in this tiny third-floor flat, so he's wearing a blue t-shirt and red shorts, and sits on the sofa with his bare feet tucked up underneath him.

But it's clear that Drew still loves music. He speaks enthusiastically about his favourite composers—Beethoven and Mozart and Tchaikovsky—who, he says, were all a little bit obsessed, as he is. When I ask him what he'd choose as his most prized possession, I'm assuming that he'll pick one of his instruments. "I suppose I should say my viola..." he muses, before suddenly remembering something else: "Hold on..." He starts rummaging in the storage underneath the coffee table. Eventually he produces a small, battered-looking Bible. The cover is curled at the edges and the spine is torn. Flicking through, the pages inside are covered in tiny notes and colourful highlights.

This, Drew says, is the Bible he was given when he first became a Christian. What makes it special to him is the message written in the front by his best friend: "Drew, my prayer for you in giving you this Bible is that you will grow in the knowledge and understanding of our awesome God. May you come back to it at all times: through times of happiness, struggle, doubt, sadness and joy. God bless you, my new brother. Matthew."

It was Matthew who first introduced Drew to Christianity. They played in a trio together at university. "Matthew invited me to an event being put on by the Christian student group. I agreed to go along in the name of openness, really. I thought of myself as a bit of a hippie, and my philosophy for life was just 'love everyone, and everything will be alright in the end'. So I thought I had to embrace all ideas. I can remember the exact room the meeting was in in the university building. The speaker was a guy called Rob, but I genuinely don't remember anything that was said—mainly because after five minutes of listening to him, I got up and started shouting abuse at him. *Literally* started shouting at him."

But why? "I wish I knew what it was that wound me up so much," Drew says, shaking his head. "I suppose it must have been something about Jesus. The point was, I didn't like it. So the next 55 minutes of this hour-long meeting was me having it out with the speaker. I don't remember anything that we said, but I do remember Rob being kind and gentle with his words."

So much for Drew's "love everyone" philosophy then? "Oh yeah, I see now what a massive hypocrite I was. But I left that meeting thinking I had won because I'd shouted the loudest. I was totally persuaded that I'd nailed it. I went off to do some practice, and about an hour later Rob and I happened to leave the building at exactly the same time. Rob said, 'Hey Drew, great to meet you today.' I remember thinking, 'No it wasn't! I was so rude to you.' Rob said, 'Listen, I'd love to meet up and chat with you more and maybe read the Bible together.' And I thought, 'Pfft, yeah OK—I'm going to convert you to *my* philosophy. I'll meet up with you and show you the right way.'"

Little did Drew imagine that six months later, having met up regularly to read the Bible, he would find himself sitting in a coffee shop with Rob having a very different conversation. Drew describes the moment he became a Christian: "Rob asked me, 'Do you think Jesus was a real person?' I said, 'Yes'. I'd done my research; I knew I could trust the Bible as a historical document—it was all legit. Then Rob asked, 'Do you believe that Jesus died on the cross for your sins?' And up to that moment, I would not have said yes. But something changed inside me in that split second. God opened my mind to see it for myself and I said, 'Yes, that's right. He did.'"

So what had changed in those six months?! "As I was reading the Bible with Rob over those months, I was so surprised by the things Jesus said. What I loved was that he was honest enough to tell me what I am actually really like. He exposes your heart. There's no hiding from the fact that Jesus thinks everybody without exception has the same problem: we've got these hearts that just spew out evil. That's what the Bible calls sin."

Drew speaks with an intensity and depth of knowledge that shows that he's put at least as much time into studying the Bible in the years since he became a Christian as he did studying music in the years before. He quotes a particular paragraph from the Bible with a startling degree of accuracy: "Jesus said, 'What comes out of a person is what defiles them. For it is from within, out of a person's heart, that evil thoughts come—

"Jesus was honest enough to tell me what I am really like."

sexual immorality, theft, murder, adultery, greed, malice, deceit, lewdness, envy, slander, arrogance and folly. All these evils come from inside and defile a person'" (Mark 7:20-23). Drew adds, "I'm yet to meet a person who can honestly look at that list and say they don't have a problem inside. And if we've got a problem with sin, we need a solution."

But what is it that makes sin such a big deal? "Well, for one thing, look at the damage it does to people. So many of the issues in the world come down to greed. But there's more to it than that. The problem is that God is God, and our hearts are rebelling against him. We don't treat him as he should be treated—as the Maker and Ruler of everything, including ourselves. Sin is that attitude of rebellion."

And the solution is...? "The cross—Jesus' death, 2000 years ago. It's like a penalty swap. The Bible says that 'the wages of sin is death'—we've earned it. And we face God's right and fair anger at our sin after death too. But Jesus died to take the penalty that I deserve. He swapped into my place and took all of God's anger at my rebellion on the cross, even though he was innocent. So now, if I accept that, my sin is fully paid for. And then the fact that Jesus came back to life again three days later shows that the cross really worked. He's not restrained by death; he beats death because he beats sin.

"That's the shock at the heart of the Bible: that Jesus Christ— the one who is the Son of God, who can walk on water and raise the dead—willingly died for me. I mean… it's outrageous. There is nothing in the world that comes close to this."

But six months into his friendship with Rob, and a few minutes into his life as a Christian, Drew didn't realise just how life-changing it all was. "At the time I didn't really quite understand why Rob and Matthew were both so excited. I had a summer of touring around the world ahead of me, and honestly, not a lot changed in the way I lived over those months. I believed that Jesus had died for my sins, but I didn't really understand what it meant to repent—to turn away from my sin and follow Jesus. I don't know how he did it, but when I came back in September, Rob somehow managed to get me to go to church and to a small group looking at the Bible together one evening each week. Once I'd started going, I was pretty consistent.

"Things changed slowly, but gradually, as I got to know Jesus better and saw his pureness and light, I realised more and more just what a sinner I really was. I remember sitting in church and thinking everyone else looked perfect, and it was as if I was just covered in mud. And I'd look down at my shoulder one day and see, 'Oh wow, I've got this hunk of dirt on me. I can take that off now; I don't need to behave like that anymore. Jesus deals with that.' And then it was like I'd look down at my foot and see that's covered in this stuff too. But that's the normal Christian life for *every* Christian. As you get to know Jesus more, he kindly shows you bit by bit just how much he's forgiven you for. And he calls you to change too. I remember Rob saying to me after about six months, 'It's time to clean up your language'. I must have seemed like such a weirdo," he laughs. "Church people are so polite, and there I was swearing at every Bible study!"

A year or so later, Drew started doing with other non-Christians exactly what Rob had done with him: reading the Bible together. "It just seemed a really obvious thing for me to do. I mean, if someone is friends with me and I'm a Christian, then why wouldn't they want to understand a little more about what makes me tick? I wanted people I knew to meet Jesus for themselves. And the way to meet Jesus is by reading the Bible."

He spent so much of his time doing this that eventually the leaders at his church suggested he give up playing music professionally and work full-time for the church instead. "It was a no-brainer," he says simply. Drew had spent over a decade

"I never fell out of love with music. I just grew to love something else more."

getting up at 5 a.m. to practise the violin, had ruthlessly pursued his music career, and had made it—and yet now he was willing to give it up. "I never fell out of love with music," he explains. "I'm still just as equally in love with music as I was. It's that I had grown to love something else more. The thing that drove me—what got me excited as I looked at my schedule for the week ahead—it wasn't the performances or practices anymore. It was telling people about Jesus as I read the Bible with them. That's what got me excited. That's what *still* gets me excited. That's what I'm obsessed with: I just want people to love Jesus."

"It just didn't make sense"

Rick's story

Rick looks like he's walking on air as he strides to meet me outside a suburban train station. He can barely contain his excitement, and it doesn't take him long to share why. This morning he and his wife have been for a 12-week scan. The baby, their first, is due in December. "It's all starting to feel real," he beams.

Despite having known Rick for less than a minute, it's hard not to feel excited for him. He has an infectious sense of enthusiasm for almost everything. He's 34 years old, works as a doctor, and describes his idea of a perfect Saturday as heading to the coast, swimming in the ocean and enjoying a big barbecue afterwards.

That last detail is particularly significant. Rick grew up in a Hindu family, which meant that for the first two decades of his life he followed a strictly vegetarian diet. Or so his mother thought. "At school, I would swap my vegetarian sandwiches— lovingly handmade by my mother and filled with all sorts of interesting salads and chunky coleslaw—for the floppy white-bread ham sandwiches that my white friends brought in. Until one day, one of those friends ran up to my mum in the schoolyard and told her how much he loved her delicious packed lunches—and the whole thing came out." Rick smiles mischievously. "She was so angry. I remember her saying, 'What on earth do you think you're doing? If your uncle or aunts or grandparents find out about this, they'll be livid!'

"Eating meat is just not what Hindus do."

So what is it that Hindus *do* do, exactly? "Hindus believe in a god that is expressed in a variety of different forms," Rick explains. "There's a goddess of money, and the god of education, and so on. We had a shrine in our house with images of different gods and goddesses that we would pray to regularly, asking them to bless us so that we would live a good life and do good to others. Because in Hinduism your good works determine what happens when you die. If you've lived a bad life, you'll be punished by being reincarnated into the animal kingdom, but if you've lived a good life, then god will bless you and reincarnate you into a better life."

Rick gestures wildly as he describes the boyhood experience of going to a big Hindu temple in north-west London for the festival of Diwali, trying to give a sense of what it's like. "It's an impressive white marble building with turrets and domes reaching up into the sky. The walls and ceilings are covered with beautifully carved details. During major festivals the air is thick with the scent of incense. Thousands of worshippers go round the shrines to various gods and goddesses, lighting candles and performing ceremonies as they ask for the gods' blessing on them and their family."

It's clear that this focus on the family was crucial to his upbringing. "In Hinduism, what I do is more than what I do—it's who I am. It forms part of your identity. And with that come expectations. You're expected to do well at school and get a successful job to reflect well on your family, your culture and your religion."

But Rick's baby is going to be born into a very different family, and have a very different upbringing than he did. For one thing, his wife is white British—Rick bucked his family's

"In Hinduism, what I do is who I am. And with that come expectations."

hopes and expectations by not marrying an Indian woman. And that wasn't the first or even main way that Rick did not walk the path laid out for him.

When asked what his greatest hopes are for his own baby, he doesn't talk about school or work or sport. He doesn't even say that he wants the child to be healthy or happy. "All my wife and I care about is that this child grows up knowing and loving the Lord Jesus." It's possibly the most serious that Rick looks in the whole time I'm with him.

How and why on earth did "the Lord Jesus" become so important to someone who was raised as a Hindu? "Never in a million years would I have guessed that this would happen," says Rick, resuming his usual expression of a broad grin. "It started when I made friends with some Christians, who encouraged me and another Buddhist friend of theirs to investigate Jesus for ourselves. This involved going to the house of a guy called Ed. A group of us would have a meal and then look at the Bible together. I went along reluctantly. In fact I missed the first few sessions altogether, and when I finally made it, I turned up late. But once I was there, I was hooked. I knew I needed to find out more. After a few weeks, to my surprise I even found myself offering to cook for Ed and the group."

But these evening discussions left Rick with more questions than answers, at least at first. "One of the things that I really, really grappled with was this: I could see that Jesus came and performed all these miracles that only God could do—therefore he was God's Son. It was clear that he was innocent—he never did anything wrong. But *why*, then, was he unjustly punished by being killed on the cross?" Rick recalls feeling "moved" as he read the account in the Bible of how Jesus was put to death. He tells me about the Roman governor, Pilate, who could find nothing that Jesus had done wrong, but sent him to be crucified anyway; the baying mob who clamoured for Jesus to be killed; the horrific physical pain that Jesus suffered as he was flogged within an inch of his life, before being hung on a cross to suffocate slowly in front of a sneering crowd; and the horrific spiritual pain that it was for Jesus, God's Son, to be separated spiritually from his heavenly Father as he died.

"I was moved but puzzled," Rick says now. "I couldn't stop asking *why*? It felt like Jesus had willingly submitted himself to all that. Even as he died, Jesus prayed for the people who were killing him, saying, 'Father, forgive them'. Why would he do that—why would he allow that?" Rick went away that evening feeling awestruck but confused.

By this stage, Rick was by no means convinced by Christianity—but equally, he knew that he needed to keep thinking it over. He went to a few more events that Ed's church was running, and eventually to church services too. He was training for the New York Marathon that year, and Ed suggested that they start training together. So on Saturday mornings they would go for long runs and talk about Christianity—and they'd focus on all the things that didn't make sense.

Rick struggles to find the words to explain what was going on inside him. He describes it as a slow, dawning realisation that he had a spiritual problem—"I came to see my own moral failures; why my best wasn't good enough; why I couldn't even meet my own goals or my parents' expectations, let alone meet the expectations that God would have. I saw that I had this problem, and it was sin."

This, says Rick, was when it "clicked". Sin was what explained the cross and answered his question of "Why?" "Because that punishment that my mum told me was coming from God when I was bad as a kid—well, Jesus took it for me on the cross, because of his love, so that I can be right with God instead. Jesus was God's Son, who became a man, lived the perfect life and died the death that can save us."

Yet still the struggles continued. Rick remembers getting particularly heated at one event when he discovered that the Bible says that only those who trust in Jesus are made right with God and can live with him in perfection when they die. Rick was outraged to be told that Gandhi—a brilliant man who changed the course of India's history—would go to hell if he didn't believe in Jesus; and that Paul of Tarsus—a first-century man who imprisoned and killed Christians just for being Christians, before becoming one himself—would go to heaven just because he did believe in Jesus. Rick left the Bible study that night feeling angry and disappointed. "It just didn't seem fair."

"But," Rick goes on, "what I hadn't understood at that stage is grace—the idea that someone is saved completely and utterly by Christ's life and death alone. None of our good works matter at all. We can do the kindest acts and have a hugely positive influence, but that will not get us to heaven and will not get us right with God, because of this problem of sin. And everyone's got that problem, regardless of who you are or where you come from or what you've done. It's only

"Christianity is about what's been done, not what you have to do."

faith in Jesus' death on the cross that deals with sin and makes you right with God." He pauses for a moment before adding firmly, "Christianity is about what's been done, not what you have to do".

By this point, Rick believed that what he had been hearing about Jesus was true—but he was a Hindu. And he knew that as Hinduism was so much a part of his family and his identity, changing faiths would be a big deal, and not just for him but also for those he loved most. Yet at the same, he knew that he couldn't be a Christian and a Hindu. It was time to make a choice. "The Bible makes demands on the way I live," he says simply, "and it's one or the other".

Eventually, he told his friend Ed that he wanted to become a Christian. Ed's response was a surprise: "Ed said to me, 'Are you sure you want to do this? Do you know what this will mean for your life? Have you thought about what your loved ones will think? There's going to be a lot of opposition. Are you absolutely sure you want this?'" Rick almost laughs as he recalls this: "But I did. I did want to do it."

And so, soon after that, Rick told his family while he was on a visit home. On Fridays his mum would perform a Hindu ceremony at the shrine in their house, which the whole family took part in. On previous occasions, Rick had been a part of it. This time, he said that he couldn't. His parents already knew that he'd been going to church, but now Rick had to explain that something was different. He'd become a Christian.

"They didn't take it particularly well," he says shortly, and without smiling. His parents were—understandably enough—disappointed and upset. They felt that Rick had thrown his whole identity back in their faces. Home became an uncomfortable place for Rick to be. He and his dad didn't speak for two months.

He's on better terms with his family now, and Rick is quick to point out that Christians from some backgrounds are actually killed by their families for their new-found faith. But it was nonetheless a really difficult few months.

"So was it worth it?" I ask.

"Absolutely," he replies with certainty, as if it is the most obvious thing in the world.

"Why?"

The grin is back. "I could give you 100 reasons why!" Rick pauses for a long moment to consider his answer, his eyebrows furrowed. "It's just… What a joy it is to know Jesus. I'm such a rebel and a screw-up. I'm a hopeless sinner, who doesn't deserve anything good from God—only his fair punishment. But Jesus took it for me. So now I don't have to try. All that pressure of trying to be good is gone. I still seek to love others, but my identity isn't in doing good things anymore. My identity is with Jesus." Rick is on a roll now—speaking with that same sense of excitement with which he announced his baby news at the start of the interview. "So now I've got this life and assurance of eternal life with Jesus for ever. So was it worth it?" he says, repeating my question back to me, before answering it with more certainty than ever. "Well, absolutely. I can't think of anything better than to love and to serve him in response to what he's done for me."

"I started reading the Bible as I got high"

Deb's story

G ood Friday 2002 in Bloemfontein, South Africa. Families were streaming into the church in the bright golden sunshine of a beautiful blue-sky morning. And outside on the street, looking desperately thin and dressed all in black, stood a woman nervously smoking cigarette after cigarette.

Sixteen years on, that woman—Deb—relives the moment: "All these shiny, happy people were walking into church with their gleaming hair and bright coloured clothes. Whereas I felt like I walked around behind my own personal prison bars. In that moment I felt this heart-aching longing to be like them. There was an innocence and a life and a light to them that I wanted. I just wished I could unlive my life and not be who I was anymore."

Even though Deb grew up in a "fairly typical" household, she had never really felt like a shiny, happy kid: "I always remember feeling that this planet wasn't my home; that somehow I'd been dropped in the wrong family. At the same time I was always worried that my parents were going to die or get divorced. I had this thing where if my dad was out late, I wouldn't go to sleep until he was home, because I thought that if I fell asleep while he was out, then he would crash and die. So I would lie awake and wait until I saw his headlights sweep into the driveway. I guess I really needed to know who was running the show, but I suspected that nobody was. I certainly didn't think that God was."

At the same time as being insecure, Deb had an "adventurous spirit"—or, as she calls it now, a rebellious streak—that liked to push the boundaries. Deb sums up her attitude to life as a young adult as, "Never say no, try everything once, sleep when you're dead". While the cool crowd played beach volleyball, Deb

"My attitude was, 'Never say no, try everything once, sleep when you're dead.'"

and her friends smoked weed on the side of the pitch. "But on the inside I was still very insecure, wanting to be liked. So I hated being single, hated being alone. And that made me stay in some very dysfunctional romantic relationships."

Deb describes life in her 20s as "crisis management". "I was always lurching from one crisis to the next. I was always threatening to derail, but because I loved my job, that meant I more or less kept things together. My friends were addicted to party drugs, and although I tried them sometimes, I never really went all in. Alcohol was more my thing."

But things did derail eventually. Deb was 30, and had just come back to South Africa after working abroad for a couple of years. "When I got home to Cape Town, I phoned up my friends and said it would be lovely to see everyone. They said 'There's a huge trance party tonight. You'll see us all there; come along.' As I walked in, one said, 'Here's some ecstasy,' and one said, 'Here's a line of coke,' and one said, 'Here's some whiskey'. That night for the first time I felt what ecstasy really did. I think it was because I was dancing. Very quickly I began going clubbing with them every weekend. Then it was Wednesdays and the weekend. Then it was Tuesdays, Wednesdays, Thursdays and the weekend."

Things spiralled further out of control when Deb got into a relationship with a guy who was involved in heroin. Eventually he persuaded her to try it. It didn't take long for her to develop an addiction. From then it was impossible to keep things together, and Deb eventually lost her two freelance jobs.

After Deb had been on heroin for over a year, and a month after losing her second freelance contract, the world was rocked by the 9/11 terror attack on the Twin Towers in New York. Deb remembers the moment: "My birthday was a few days before. I'd had a whole weekend partying with all my friends, and I'd had literally every single kind of drug possible. By the 11th I was just starting to recover. Someone messaged me to say 'Switch on the TV'. So I did. I can remember standing on my futon in my dressing gown with my eyes glued to the TV, just watching the replay. First one tower, then the next. And I could hear this voice to the side of my head, inside my ear, saying, 'You see that, my girl, you see that? You're going down.' I just knew that on the screen in front of me I was seeing where my life was going: destruction. Absolute destruction."

It was the shock Deb needed to get her out of Cape Town to kick the heroin habit. She and her boyfriend arranged to house-sit for some his family members in the middle of nowhere so they could go cold turkey together.

Deb audibly groans as she relives the agony of coming off heroin: "I spent three days lying in my room wanting to die. Then the first time I ventured out of the room, I just sat on the couch in the living room. I couldn't walk for very long, couldn't sit up for very long, I was so physically weak.

"And I remember seeing the REM song on the TV, 'Everybody Hurts', and I just thought, 'Yes, absolutely'. Now I was sober, I could see the horror of who I was and what I had done. I had nothing. I'd sold everything I had to get out of Cape Town—all

"I thought, 'What is there worth living for?'"

I had with me was my two cats, my computer and a backpack. I hadn't spoken to my family in months. I'd cut myself off from my friends. I had trashed my career. I'd lost any sense that I'd achieved anything with my life. Here I was, 32 years old and absolutely finished and washed out. There was a deep sense of shame. And I thought, 'What's the point? What is there worth living for?' I started looking for a way to end my life, but I didn't know how."

After two months of total misery, one of the companies Deb used to work for invited her back to Cape Town for a week to finish off a project. She arranged to stay in a friend's flat while he was away. But the first thing she did when she got there was to call the dealer. "This guy did delivery, which was convenient. I was looking for matches to light a candle so that I could 'chase the dragon': you burn a little bit of the heroin powder on tinfoil and inhale the fumes. I was scrabbling in this drawer, and I found a little blue New Testament. As I got high, I decided to start reading it. I'd always mocked the Bible, but I'd never actually read it. Even though I was definitely heroin-hazed, I couldn't put it down."

What she read was deeply disturbing: "I was just flicking through, but wherever I looked, I saw condemnation. I didn't see anything about a God of love. I didn't see anything about acceptance. The thing was, I already knew I had done a bad thing with the heroin. I knew that it was bad on a social level. I knew that what I had done would bring shame to my family. But what dawned on me as I read that little New Testament was how deeply I had sinned against God. It was sin; it wasn't just an embarrassment—I had done wrong before God. I had taken this life he had given me and utterly driven it into the ground. I owed him an account for how I'd lived. And so I realised that I couldn't end my life—because if I died, I would stand before him. Death was no longer a way out—it was actually a way into much deeper trouble."

This made sobering up for the second time at the end of her week in Cape Town even more excruciating: "I was lying curled up on a mattress, unable to move, in absolute physical agony, like before. Only now I was in absolute soul anguish before God too. It felt like every single cell of my body was on fire. Like I was in the deepest, darkest place. It felt like I was lying beyond where even God could reach. It really was a sense of the outermost…" She pauses and sighs as she searches for the words: "Just aloneness and unreachableness".

Now, as she looks back, Deb says something startling: "It wasn't the heroin that got me into trouble with God".

So what was it? "The problem was my heart, which insisted that God was of no account, and that I could live my life however I wanted. Before I went near any substances, I was just as ugly a person on the inside as I became on the outside. I was guilty of pride; I was guilty of selfishness; I told lies. I organised my universe to suit myself. So in a sense, the outer problem of a drug addiction was easier to deal with than the inner problem: that attitude which is hard towards God and puts itself first. I'd say now that I'm actually kind of grateful for the heroin addiction. Had my life not gone so spectacularly off the tracks, I might still be under the illusion that I was actually a good person. Because you can have a respectable job and a respectable family, but if you live without reference to God—never thinking about him, being completely indifferent to him—that's sin. That's an offence to God, because he made us and he loves us and wants a relationship with us."

Not that Deb knew any of this as she slunk into the back of church on that sunny Good Friday morning in 2002. By that stage she was living in Bloemfontein (hundreds of miles from Cape Town), sleeping on her brother's couch, and had managed to get herself a part-time job. She had heard colleagues in the office talking about Easter, and felt compelled to go to church. But when she got there, she felt extremely uncomfortable: "I went in eventually, and sat right at the back, on the end of the pew, near the door, so that if anybody spoke to me, I could just make a quick getaway. As the service started I had no idea what to expect. There was some singing, and they said that it was Good Friday, the day that Christians remember Jesus' death on the cross. Then they read from the Bible."

Deb was riveted by the whole account of Jesus' arrest and trial and crucifixion. She remembers the scene as he was hung on the cross to die being described: "Those who passed by hurled insults at [Jesus], shaking their heads and saying, '… Come down from the cross, if you are the Son of God!' In the same way the chief priests, the teachers of the law and the elders mocked him. 'He saved others,' they said, 'but he can't save himself! He's the king of Israel! Let him come down now from the cross, and we will believe in him'" (Matthew 27:39-42).

Deb adds, "I remember just being drawn into being right there and knowing I was one of the scoffers, one of those who mocked him. I started crying because I could see myself in all of that. I was sobbing. Then it got to the part where Jesus, right before he died, cried out, 'My God, my God, why have you

"I was just… overjoyed. From that point onward there was no sense of guilt."

forsaken me?' And somehow, at that point I realised that Jesus was forsaken—abandoned by God the Father—instead of me. He was being punished in my place. I had lived my whole life with this sense of homelessness—it was a fear of abandonment, really. And since coming off heroin, it felt like I was in a living hell. And at that point I knew that Jesus had headed into hell and plucked me out. He was forsaken so that I wasn't. He was abandoned so that I wasn't." She shakes her head, almost in disbelief. "I was just… overjoyed. Still sobbing, but at peace. From that point onward there was no sense of guilt, because I knew Christ had dealt with my sin for me. So when I walked out of that church, as those huge wooden doors were pushed open, I walked out knowing that I was God's daughter."

Towards the end of our time together, Deb's own daughter comes into the room, wanting the reassurance of a quick hug before dashing out again. It's a reminder of how much has changed for the woman chain-smoking outside that church. Deb and her husband have two children, both of whom are adopted. "People always say that they're little mini-me's of my husband and me—it's bizarre," she laughs. Deb has stolen herself away to the attic to speak with me, hiding from the chaos of construction work going on downstairs. She and her husband have set up a little Christian school in their home, and are turning some rooms into classrooms. It is, Deb admits, a strange time for a family like theirs to be investing in South Africa: "People are emigrating in their droves because of the political unrest here". So why stay?

It comes back to that Good Friday in 2002—or rather, what happened two days later, on Easter Sunday. "We met on a little hillside for an outdoor service with the sun rising. And there was singing outside and the Bible was read, and there was very much a sense of life. It was such a joy."

Deb explains that what gets her through tough times is one of the claims at the heart of Christianity—that after Jesus died, he didn't stay dead. The Bible says that on the Sunday morning after his execution, his followers found his tomb empty, and then met Jesus for themselves, alive again; and that after forty days of meeting and interacting with his followers, Jesus returned to heaven. "Jesus is my risen Lord. He is alive. He is reigning as King and is with me by the presence of his Holy Spirit." She pauses. " I think it probably speaks to that desire of mine as a very young child to know that someone is running the show. Someone *is* in charge—Jesus Christ! And one day he's coming back to draw everything together and put everything right, and I will be with him in eternity face to face. This is what gives me comfort and joy when things are hard."

And this, she says, is what helps her make sense of South Africa today. "My husband and I have such a sense that Christ our Lord wants us here—that he has stationed us here for this time in South African history. His kingdom is worth more to us than having a secure pension fund or knowing that life is safe. We are Christ's servants, and we will remain posted where we are, because what's coming is far more glorious that we can ever imagine."

She's glad she stubbed out the final cigarette, and headed into that church, on Good Friday in 2002.

"I was scared of how life would change"

Nicky's story

When one of Nicky's older sisters became a Christian, she sent Nicky her "testimony"—the story of how it happened. "I remember reading it and thinking, 'Oh no, she's completely lost the plot'."

Almost two decades later, and Nicky is sharing her own story of how she "lost the plot" herself. We're in the church building where it happened. She doesn't live in the area anymore, but coming into this church, she says, feels like coming home.

Not that she's always felt that way. She remembers her first impressions on coming here with her sisters before she became a Christian: "I loved the singing, but otherwise it was all a bit weird. People got out these notebooks during the sermon to jot things down in, and I was thinking, 'Right, the Bible is open, people are writing, and the person at the front is just not stopping talking'. Very strange. The church thing didn't sit with me. I felt like my community—my 'church', if you like—were the people I hung out with. I loved music, drama and going out, and I felt like that was what my soul needed rather than anything else.

"I guess I didn't think I needed church or Christianity."

Nicky had a conventional, happy childhood, growing up in a "very sweet village" as the youngest of four girls. "Three sisters! How was *that*?" I ask. (I have one. And it's enough.) "Oh, it wasn't too complicated," she laughs. But on reflection, she realises that maybe it was at least a little bit complicated: "I suppose there was that constant comparison. And as I got older, I just wanted to be different to my sisters. They were all very good girls, and I didn't want to be good. I loved drinking and smoking and doing everything that I knew they didn't. I was just trying to be my own person." When, one by one, her older sisters became Christians after they had left home, Nicky thought they were crazy: "I thought of myself as more independent than they were. So while I was fine with them believing what they wanted—you know, whatever made them happy—I knew I definitely didn't need 'religion'. But they kept trying to tell me about Jesus. They were pretty nice about it, but it made me uncomfortable."

There was one particular conversation that stuck in Nicky's mind: "My sister and I were talking about Christian things and she got quite upset and said, 'The problem is, Nicky, unless you believe this you're going to go to hell'. I think she'd got to the point where she'd tried being soft and gentle, we'd had lots of conversations, she'd given me stuff to read—but I wasn't taking it seriously. After she said that, I totally closed down. I thought, 'Well, if that's what it's about, then I'm never going to become a Christian'."

Then a major terror attack hit the headlines. By this point, Nicky was working as a teacher: "I was at school and it was a really busy day. But I remember putting on the news in the classroom at the end of the day, watching the footage and feeling… confused. Just thinking, 'How could anybody do that?' It totally blew my mind. I remember that night it was going round and round and round and round in my head. A few days later, a friend went to a church to sit and think and see if he could find some answers in the peace there. And I just thought, 'What's the point of that?' I couldn't make head nor tail of what was going on in the world, and I was angry."

It was in the wake of this terror attack that Nicky's sister invited her to a course her church were running for people who

"I was angry that my sisters could believe in a God who had let that happen."

wanted to investigate Christianity. Nicky had turned down similar invitations in the past. But now, she had a reason to accept: "I was so cross with my sisters—that they could believe in a God who had let that happen. If there was a God, why didn't he stop it? So I thought I would go once, to tell all those Christians how stupid they were."

But once became twice, and Nicky kept going along—mainly because her sister was pregnant, and she liked having a reason to see her week by week and bond with the bump.

Yet slowly, the things she heard started to have an impact too: "We had these booklets as part of the course. It's really funny now when I look at it, because the back pages are full of questions that I had. I didn't know anything about who Jesus was, so I had a lot of questions. But as time went on a lot of them weren't really questions I cared about—they were a barrier I put up because I didn't want to believe what I was hearing. But at the same time, I was really curious. And the Christians leading the course were really nice—so lovely and so patient. And bit by bit things started to piece together in my mind. It was like Jesus walked off the pages of the Bible. The more I read it, what had seemed like a completely foreign language began to make sense. Jesus was starting to figure in my mind as a real person. I loved how when he said that something would happen, it happened. He was totally trustworthy and he loved people. I wanted to be part of that.

"But I also didn't want to be a part of it. It scared me thinking about what would have to change if I was to follow him."

At the end of the course, Nicky's sister gave her testimony to the group, explaining why she was a Christian. Nicky was invited to follow it up by giving her "half testimony"— explaining why she was interested but still not decided.

She went on to do the course for a second time when the church ran it again in the new year. "This time, I was more open to stuff. I was beginning to read the Bible more myself—just a little bit in the mornings or whenever. I was becoming more and more curious, and going along to different events with my sisters at their churches. I got to the stage where I understood the gospel—the message about Jesus—and I thought it was real, but still didn't want to commit to it. I remember meeting a Christian friend of my sister's outside church one Sunday. He asked me how things were going and I explained. He said to me, 'Nicky, it's like you're dangling on the edge of a cliff by a piece of rope that bit by bit is just starting to go. So you have to make the choice to grab hold of the rope and pull yourself up. God's got you, but unless you make that choice the rope is gonna break.'"

So why was she holding back? "I was scared of what that would mean for me, and what people would say and how life would change. I felt I would have to give up all the things I considered fun. And I knew that if I became a Christian, it was likely that I would lose friends—I didn't want to be lonely. I knew from the conversations I'd had with my friends about my sisters that they would think I was a hypocrite if I became a Christian too."

The turning point came when Nicky heard a sermon based on these words of Jesus: "Enter through the narrow gate. For wide is the gate and broad is the road that leads to destruction, and many enter through it. But small is the gate and narrow the road that leads to life, and only a few find it" (Matthew 7:13-14).

Whereas previously Nicky had thought people were weird for writing notes during a sermon, now she was the one with her pen out: "As the preacher was talking, I started drawing on the back of a service sheet: the narrow gate leading to a narrow road and a broad gate leading to a broad road. And I just knew that right there, in that moment, it was like I was at the crossroads. I had a choice. I could carry on down the broad road, living life my own way. In some ways that looked like the more comfortable, more enjoyable option. But I knew it ultimately led to a dark, fearful place—hell. That word just kept coming up. And it's not a made-up place. It's real. Or I could choose this very brilliant, bright narrow road that led to Jesus. He's the one who makes sense of life now, and who gives eternal life in the future.

"As I listened to that sermon, it became absolutely crystal clear that I had to choose one or the other. So a couple of days later, I stepped onto the narrow road. I prayed to Jesus and just said, 'I'm sorry. I know I've stuffed up life by myself. I need you to forgive me. And even though I'm scared, I know you've got me and I know you love me and I know this is the right choice.'"

That, says Nicky, is what being a Christian is all about: following Jesus. But not like you might take a vague interest in a celebrity: "It's like a friend. In order to get to know my friends more, I want to spend time with them. So the way I get to know Jesus more is by spending time with him. I do that by reading

"Following Jesus gives me the confidence to be who I really am."

his word and speaking to him in prayer and spending time with his family, with other Christians, as part of a church. Jesus isn't a figment of my imagination. I really relate to him. He gave his life for me. That's the most amazing thing that anybody could ever do for somebody. Why wouldn't I want to spend time getting to know him and enjoying his company?"

But how much fun did she have to give up when she became a Christian? "I still have fun now!" she protests, laughing. Then she adds more seriously, "I don't want this to sound judgmental; it's just how it was for me. Before I became a believer, my life centred around getting drunk. I'd spend most nights at bars or clubs, with a view to meeting a guy that I could have sex with, and who would hopefully end up as a boyfriend. To me, for a long while, that was 'fun', but looking back, it was all kind of a mask. I was hiding: trying to be someone that deep down I wasn't. I was trying too hard and, if I'm honest about it... I genuinely wasn't happy. But now I know Jesus loves me unconditionally, and following him gives me the confidence to be who I really am. He makes me more myself, more the person I'm meant to be. It sounds strange, but the way he makes me into the person I'm meant to be is by changing me to be more like him—bit by bit, day by day. But I'm definitely still a work in progress!"

Telling her friends about her decision to become a Christian was as hard as Nicky expected it to be. "The first few times I met up with my friends, I ended up getting drunk with them because it seemed normal. But gradually I didn't feel comfortable doing that anymore, and that brought a little bit of distance into some of my relationships. But I knew the only way I could live as a Christian was to be true to who Jesus wanted me to be. At first I was kind of apologetic for becoming a Christian when I told people, because I was afraid of what they would say. I remember meeting up with one friend from school and she asked me, 'So, how are your Bible-bashing sisters?' And I had to say, 'Actually, I've become one!' I don't think she could quite believe it."

Those early days and months as a Christian were exciting too: "There'd been so much of a build-up to becoming a Christian, and now suddenly there was this kind of relief that I'd finally said yes to Jesus. It's funny," she says, laughing. "That first day after I became a Christian I was in this bubble of excitement. And then I had a really terrible day at work. I left earlier than I would normally, and I bumped into this girl who lived near me as I was crossing the road. It turned out that she had become a Christian the day before too. She'd left her keys at work and couldn't get into her house. So we'd both had a really bad first day as Christians! We ended up going for coffee and having a really good chat. We realised that it probably wasn't a coincidence that we'd met!"

Whereas Nicky had read the Bible before, now the way that she read it changed: "I just remember being so excited about reading it every day. When I was reading the Bible before I became a Christian, I was trying so hard to prove it was wrong. But now as I was reading it, I just genuinely wanted to know what it said."

Now, 16 years on, I ask Nicky what her younger self would make of her life now. "I think she would probably be quite amazed that I've stuck at being a Christian. Life hasn't turned out how I thought it would. I thought I'd be married with kids by now, but I'm not…" she says, her tone suddenly revealing a more vulnerable side beneath the bubbly exterior: "I've had

"Life hasn't turned out how I thought – but I wouldn't take that decision back."

a really tough time recently. I've been off work for a bit with anxiety and depression. Life can be hard. There are times when I think back to that decision at the crossroads and wonder, would it be easier to go back down onto the wide road? But I can't, and deep down I don't want to either. I can't leave the truth of who Jesus is. I can't forget what he's done for me. I know that he's got me. Even when it feels like I'm in a pit, however bad I'm feeling and however dark things are, it's like there's still this tiny shaft of light," she says, raising her hand with her fingers pinched together and starting to smile again, "and that light is Jesus.

"That's the amazing thing about God. Once he's got you, he just doesn't let you go."

"I knew I had to do something to get my life together"

David's story

The year 1990 was David's *annus horribilis*. In that one horrible year, almost everything that could go wrong did go wrong.

His marriage had broken down a few years before. At the start of 1990 his ex-wife made the decision to move abroad to be closer to her family, and took their two young children with her. "That was obviously incredibly painful," says David, "and it kind of started a chain of disastrous events".

They'd sold their house when they separated and split the money. David used the little money he was left with to buy a tiny flat in a commuter town, where he tried to piece life back together. "But it was bad timing. There was a big recession in 1990, and the company I was working for went bust. It was inevitable, really. The whole business was based around selling office furniture—and the last thing anybody does in a recession is redecorate their office! The rest of the year was a downward spiral of periods of unemployment mixed with a string of jobs, each of which was a backward step."

By the end of the year, David had been made redundant three times, and the financial consequences were dire. "I couldn't pay the mortgage on the flat I had bought, and so the bank repossessed it and sold it." House prices had fallen during

"I was divorced, unemployed and without a permanent home. It was a really bad time."

the recession, which meant that David ended up in negative equity—tens of thousands in debt and with no home.

"I was divorced, unemployed and without a permanent home. And because I didn't have any money, I stopped socialising. It was a really bad time, to be honest. I became severely depressed and at my lowest I was probably suicidal. It was just the fact that I loved my kids that saved me from…"

It's at this moment, as David quietly recounts those dark days, that we're interrupted. We're having lunch at the cafe of the church community centre where David now works as the manager, and someone comes over to the table to give him an envelope. In the course of the interview another person needs his help with something in the office. Someone else rings his iPhone—twice—until they get through to him. When we're interrupted for the fourth time, David shrugs his shoulders and says with a smile, "Welcome to my world".

While David is in the office averting an IT disaster, a member of staff brings over the food to our table (a tuna salad and

Coke Zero for him). I ask her how she would describe David. "Oh, he's incredibly hardworking," is the first thing she says. "Organised, approachable. He's a very good boss actually, because he's not on my back the whole time, but I know I can go to him if I need help, and he will always listen and back me up. He's very focused—he just gets on with doing what needs to be done."

It seems a pretty accurate description. After all, this is a man whose sporting hero is the '80s English footballer Kevin Keegan, "because he wasn't the most naturally gifted player but you could tell that he trained really hard get where he was". David's musical hero, for the record, is Bruce Springsteen.

As a kid growing up in a working-class Jewish family, David spent a lot of his youth in a place not unlike the community centre he now runs—at a youth club in the east end of the city. "It was set up for poor Jewish kids in the 1890s by wealthy Jewish benefactors. By the 1950s and 60s when I was going, they had a big three-storey building with a theatre and space for lots of sports and activities. It was an amazing place. That club really shaped me—it gave me a great sense of community and Jewish identity."

David's parents were not particularly religious. The family would celebrate the major festivals, but being "Jewish" was more of a cultural identity than a religion to follow strictly. By the time David left home at 18, he "definitely, definitely didn't do God. I had no interest in it. Playing football was what dominated my weekends."

But two decades later David found himself alone and desperate, having lost his job, his home, and his family in the course of that one horrible year. "I knew I had to do something to get myself together. I didn't have any money for a therapist, so I went to a book shop and looked in the self-help section. I bought a book off the shelf and read the first few chapters, which had these little psychological tips, and they seemed to work a bit. Then one Sunday evening in December, as I was reading it in my bedroom, I came to a chapter on 'the power of prayer'. I didn't know it, but the book had some content that was Christian, mixed with other self-help techniques. In this particular chapter, it talked about the fact that you can pray to God personally and tell him what's on your mind. I remember thinking it all sounded a bit weird. In Judaism when you pray, you mainly recite set prayers in Hebrew—so this idea that you could actually speak to God as a person was very strange. But because I was desperate to do something to turn my life around, and because everything I'd read so far in the book had been quite useful, I thought, 'Well OK, let's try this then'."

But David got a lot more than he bargained for. "The book said to just tell God what's in your heart. So I sat back in my chair... and that's when I had a vision of Jesus."

Wait... he had what?! "I know, I know, it sounds weird when people say stuff like that," he says quickly. "But it really happened. I wasn't dreaming, I wasn't on drugs, I hadn't been drinking. It was so real and so powerful—and I know for sure it happened because my whole life changed from that moment on."

But how did he know it was Jesus? "It's like... how do you know you're in love? You just know. That's the only way I can describe it. I just knew it was Jesus. I saw his head hovering just above me, and it was against this kind of glowing background. And the thing that struck me was that he was smiling at me... So that was the vision. It was brief, but it was real," David says firmly.

"Just after it happened I was really scared—I thought that I was cracking up. But then shortly after that, I just had this warm feeling flowing through me. It was kind of as if Jesus was putting his arm around my shoulder and saying, 'Don't worry, everything is going to be alright now'. For the rest of the evening I basked in the warm glow of this feeling. I felt better than I had done, not just since the beginning of this horrible year but for a long, long time."

The next morning, David went to work. "I'd recently started yet another new job, where I'd met this guy called Steve. We had hit it off instantly—he was just such a great guy. Steve was a Christian—he was always very open about that, but not in a pushy way. So I couldn't wait to tell him about this amazing thing that had happened to me. But when I got to work, before I said anything to him, Steve said, 'What's happened to you?' I said, 'What do you mean?' He said, 'You've looked so down since I've known you, but today you're almost glowing. What's happened?' I told him about my experience the night before and asked him what he thought it meant. He said, 'Well, I think that maybe God's trying to tell you something'. 'But how do I know what that is?' I asked. Steve explained that the way God speaks to people is through the Bible, and suggested that I try reading it. So I asked Steve if he would come with me at lunchtime to buy one. He said no. Instead, he went to his desk and brought out a brand new Bible from his drawer. He said that he had been praying for me and had felt compelled to buy a Bible for me a couple of weeks before."

David started by reading the New Testament. The first book he came across was therefore Matthew's Gospel. As a Jew, what struck him was how Jewish it all felt. "Lots of people assume that Jesus was a Christian, but a Christian is someone who follows Jesus. In fact, Jesus was born as a Jew, in ancient Israel.

Matthew's Gospel starts with a list of Jesus' ancestry that goes right back to centuries before, and to Jewish heroes like King David and Abraham. So as I was reading, I felt very drawn to it. It had the ring of truth—it definitely didn't sound like it was

"I'm Jewish, not a Christian. What am I getting myself into?"

all made up. But at the same time I thought, 'I'm Jewish—and I didn't get into all this to become a Christian'."

Soon, David had read the whole New Testament. Steve gave him a piece of paper on which he'd scribbled the phone number of a friend of a friend, Bernie, who lived near to David and was willing to meet up with him and talk through some of his questions.

The piece of paper sat on David's bedside cabinet for a long time.

"I kept thinking, 'I'm Jewish; I'm not a Christian. What am I getting myself into?'" Eventually, he took the plunge and made the call.

Bernie was a doctor, a scientist and a Christian. He invited David round to his house for a meal. "He said to me, 'David, you've obviously had this very emotional experience of a vision. But you're clearly an intelligent, thoughtful person. It seems to me like you probably want some more proof about who Jesus is and what he did.' He invited me to come to a series of sessions looking at Jesus. He was just brilliant. It all became really clear."

By this point, David was sure that what he was reading about Jesus was true—but he was still reluctant at the idea of giving up his Jewish identity to become a Christian. The turning point came when he watched the video testimony of the 1960s pop singer Helen Shapiro, who also came from a Jewish background, and who had become a Christian. "It really filled in a gap for me. I realised that I was Jewish because I was born into a Jewish family—I'll always have that cultural identity. But I can be a Christian too, because being a Christian is ultimately about following Jesus. It's not about giving up your culture. It's about putting him first."

So what does that actually mean in daily life? "Now I'm a Christian, my life is not about me—it's about him. That means I try and live in a way that is obedient to Jesus. One of the key things about living as a Christian is serving people—putting others before yourself. So that's what I aim to do."

David's keen to underline that there's a difference between seeing that Christianity is true and actually becoming a Christian. "It comes down to commitment," he explains. "If you're going to come out and say you're Christian, you need to be committed to it. Because it does mean your life is going to change." David made that commitment in February 1991—just three months after he'd bought that book: "Bernie asked me to pray a simple prayer with him. I told God that I wanted to turn away from my sin and asked Jesus to come into my life."

Soon after, David got baptised—in Bernie's swimming pool. He started reading the Bible regularly and became part of a church. After a while, he was asked to become a children's Sunday School teacher. He got back into employment and worked his way up to the level he'd been at before his crisis. Later, he met another new Christian, a lady called Heather—they fell in love and got married.

Yet David makes clear that becoming a Christian "doesn't make all your problems go away. But it will give you an entirely different perspective on life. This life is temporary; but Jesus is eternal. And he is with me through all life's stresses and strains."

And David needed to hold on to that—because his commitment to Christ came at a cost. "It was a big step to tell my family. I didn't face outright hostility; it was more that they thought I was really, really strange. They couldn't quite believe it. It was hardest for my mother—she came from a generation that lived through the Holocaust, and in her mind I was almost becoming a traitor to our people."

Some of his family and friends still think he's a bit strange—not least because after working at this church community centre for almost 15 years, he and his wife recently made the decision to retire. They plan to uproot their lives and move to a town 200 miles north of here. They've sold their flat and are going to leave behind most of their friends, so that they can be part of a new church that is just starting up. "People who don't get Jesus don't get this decision," he says. "They think we're crazy! But we're so excited—I can't wait to use my retirement to serve Jesus and serve other people."

"I thought Christians were stupid bigots"

Rachel's story

Rachel asks to meet in a fried chicken restaurant. "It's basically my favourite food ever."

The restaurant is a stylish place, with quirky paintings of chickens on the wall that look down on the customers eating their deep-fried counterparts. Rachel's brought along her best friend, Sarah, and the waitress who brings the menus suggests getting some dishes to share. But Rachel is adamant: "I need my own chicken—I don't want to share!" She has long brown hair, thick glasses, and a slightly off-beat sense of humour that makes her fun to be around; as she looks at the menu she makes a joke about ordering chicken breasts, which she later decides is too trashy to include in this write-up.

The joke works, it turns out, because it was Rachel's sexuality that was one of the reasons she became totally opposed to Christianity as a teenager. "I didn't grow up in a Christian home at all," she explains. "So I guess I started life neutral towards

Christianity, and then, as I moved into my high school years, I became more opposed to it. The main reason was that I saw it as being for stupid people. That was mostly because the Christians I was talking to were only about 14 years old. It's not really fair to make a judgment about a huge intellectual tradition based on the reasoning of children. But then," she shrugs, "we're not always fair, are we?

"Then, as I was about 16, I started to understand my sexuality more. I'd already had some sexual relationships with men— well, high-school boys, really. But as I started to be attracted to women and then act on those attractions, I was like, 'Oh, this is where my heart is. The reason stuff with boys felt out of place was because it's not my place.' I gradually started to own that identity more and more. I knew from the culture that Christianity was against homosexuality. So by the time I was 18, I had concluded that Christians were both stupid and bigots."

It's clear that Rachel is a woman who thinks deeply about things—which was part of the reason her teenage self was so excited to go to Yale. "I was so looking forward to being at one of America's most prestigious universities—I imagined that Yale was going to be a great place for me. But the first thing that happened was that I realised that, actually, most people are much smarter than me. That shot me down. And then my girlfriend broke up with me—she was this girl from high school that I felt totally in love with. So I was kind of in a tailspin. Then one day in philosophy class they were talking about René Descartes' proof of God…" Rachel waves a hand to show that the details of this particular philosophical argument are not important, "Anyway, I was curious about the existence of God… but at the same time I was ashamed about that curiosity. So I would secretly look up things about faith and Christianity on my computer. What I read about Jesus online was much more compelling than what I'd expected. So I was drawn in by

"I was drawn in by Jesus – but at the same time, my sexuality was a big barrier."

this different Jesus—but at the same time, my sexuality was a big barrier. I knew that I wanted to marry a woman some day, and I knew that Christianity wasn't OK with that."

Rachel looked for a way to square "this different Jesus" and her sexuality: "I went and talked to two girls I knew who identified as Christians and were dating each other. They were like, 'Yeah, you can totally be a Christian and go out with a woman'. They gave me a bunch of information to read at home. I was so excited. I so wanted to believe it.

"But then I pulled up the Bible on my computer and checked the quotes they were using to make their arguments that it was all OK, and I realised, 'This doesn't add up. This is not what these sections of the Bible are really saying.'

"I knew then that there was not a way to reconcile my sexuality and Jesus."

But somehow, Rachel couldn't shake off her interest in Jesus. One day, she was in the room of a college friend and noticed a book on her shelf with an intriguing title: *Mere Christianity* by C.S. Lewis, the university-professor-cum-children's-author who wrote the Chronicles of Narnia stories. "The title grabbed me, but there was no way I was going to admit that I was interested in Christianity by asking to borrow it. So I stole it." As she secretly read it, she had a dawning realisation which she describes as: "Oh my goodness—God is real, and I am in a lot of trouble. Because not only is he real; he is perfect, and I am incredibly *imperfect*." But there was an element of hope there too, she says: "I understood for the first time that Jesus

"I can't pretend the Bible is not true just because it is inconvenient."

had come to place himself as a kind of wall between God's wrath—his right and fair anger at my sin—and me. I knew that if I trusted in Jesus, I was going to be saved. Now, did I understand the full implications of that? Certainly not. But I knew that I could be somehow be connected to Jesus and saved from God's anger.

"I remember thinking, 'Well, I like to drink a lot, I like the excessive parts of my lifestyle, I like to sleep with women—and all those things will have to go out the window. But it is stupid to pretend like what the Bible is saying isn't true just because it's inconvenient. I need to take this deal because I'm never going to get a deal like this again.' I had a sense that I needed to pray, and so I just talked to God right then."

A couple of days later, Rachel ran into the Christian student group on campus. "I had a ton of questions, obviously. I didn't know anything! They were very good in giving me a Bible, showing me how to pray, taking me to church. The female friends who drew around me became very close to me, helping me fight through the sexual temptation and sexual failure that came. It became pretty clear to me after a little while that my attractions toward women hadn't just gone when I became a Christian. Those first few years were littered with bad decisions. I was committed to Christ, but then I would choose a sexual relationship and get stuck in these cycles… But my friends would lovingly keep calling me back to what I believed in."

But it's time to address the elephant in the room in all this. Why can't Jesus just accept people the way they are? Why is it the case that for Rachel, as a lesbian, "there was not a way to reconcile [her] sexuality and Jesus"?

Rachel chews thoughtfully as she considers this question. "He does accept who people are, in the sense that he made them and loves them. God designed everything in his creation to reveal who he is and to bless us. That includes sex. It's not that he looked down from the sky one day and said, 'Oh no, look at what those humans are doing with their bodies—I need to regulate this with some rules!' No, sex was God's idea, including the pleasure that goes along with it.

"And I can trust him—he's not saying no to my desires towards women in an arbitrary or a mean way. If something seems good to me, it's hard to imagine why it doesn't seem good to God. But it's like God says, *I define what is good. I've designed sex to work a certain way, and when you use it opposite to the design, it wrecks you and it wrecks the gift and it wrecks your ability to understand me. The reason I care enough to say this is because I'm for you and I love you.*"

But while insisting that what Jesus says is good, Rachel readily admits that the church has often acted badly towards LGBT people: "If people think the church is homophobic, they're not totally wrong. In the past Christians have acted cruelly in a lot of ways. There's been a lot of name-calling and shaming and sometimes physical abuse. Sadly, that's sometimes still the case.

The church has a responsibility to apologise for its mistakes and to do better.

"The truth is that God says we're *all* created equal and we are *all* sexually broken—every one of us, whether we're gay or straight, needs the power of Christ to become whole again. Christians are wrong if they treat homosexuality like it's worse sin than heterosexual sin. So yes, the church has said and done things to object to—but not Jesus himself. He's the one who matters."

OK—but how could you just give up such an important part of your identity, something that had been so fundamental to your sense of self for so long? "Well," Rachel says slowly, "it would definitely be tragic to give up something that valuable for something that is less valuable. And it would also be tragic to pretend like this real part of my life, my sexuality, is less than it is. But Jesus is more precious than even that very deep part of me, because of his great love. And…" she pauses for a moment with a smile, "that sounds really weird if you're not a Christian, right? But the Bible talks about a Christian's relationship with Christ being something we should be able to die for because it's so precious. And celibacy and singleness are not death," she says frankly. "Not having sex or not experiencing a romantic relationship is a severe thing, but I'd be willing to give up even more than that. In fact, giving up things is a very normal part of the Christian life. There are lots of people who give up sex, who give up their bodies, who give up their money. And you don't really do it out of obligation—you do it out of love. You're captured by Christ's love, and it drives you to do things that you never thought possible before, because Jesus gives you this sense of security and purpose and an ultimate destination."

Rachel says that this promise of eternal life changes the way she approaches life now: "Previously I lived as if this life is the only life I have. I was told that I need to maximise it, because I've got maybe 80 years, and for several of them I'll be frail, so the ones when I'm healthy I need to take full advantage of—and that includes sex. So that's what I pursued. And, yeah, some of the sex was very good, but some of it was pretty crappy and disappointing and emotionally a let-down and not all the things

"Now I don't feel like I have to squeeze everything out of this life in order to find joy."

it was cracked up to be. It was a hugely mixed bag. But the thing is, I don't have to squeeze everything out of this life in order to find joy. Because God made me and knows me, I can trust him that living his way will bring me joy. And it has led to my joy. How would I have ever known how much joy he brings if I didn't trust him and take this step?

"And anyway, my trust wasn't based on ridiculous things," she adds, thinking back to her decision to become a Christian at Yale. "I did a lot of research on the historical reliability of the resurrection. The reason that most people aren't Christians is either because they think that Jesus isn't really real or that he isn't really worth it. But Jesus is both—really real and really worth it. He once said that 'no one who has left home or brothers or sisters or mother or father or children or fields for me and the gospel will fail to receive a hundred times as much in this present age … and in the age to come eternal life' (Mark 10:29-30). I have absolutely found that to be true. Yes, I gave up some major things and some significant sexual relationships—but God has heaped upon me beautiful and good things in their place."

Rachel's friendship with Sarah is a case in point—as dinner continues, there's an easy back-and-forth of jokes and conversation across the table. They share a love for softball and college football, and for Rachel's four-year-old daughter: "Sarah is like a third parent to her," Rachel says.

Which brings us to the final twist in Rachel's story: how she met the father of her daughter—her husband.

"So... how did you end up married to a *man*?" I ask, slightly baffled.

"Oh, I know..." she replies sympathetically. She accepts that many people find this part of the story strange, or offensive. "When I met Andrew, we both had a crush on the same girl—so it was definitely not love at first sight. Life took us separate ways, but then months later he reached out to me out of the blue and we reconnected. And then I started to get the feeling that he liked me. And I thought, 'Oh no'. But I had this sense from God that I should just give it a try. As we were dating, I saw that we made a good team and wanted the same things in life.

"But I had to wrestle with the fact that the attraction I felt to him was not the same as with my girlfriends. That felt more like butterflies and fireworks," she says, waving her hand above her head. "My attraction to Andrew seemed like a quiet little thing that was real but much more vulnerable"—she cups her hands in front of her as if she were holding a tiny animal—"and I wondered if I was fooling myself. I spent a lot of time talking to my friends and praying about it, and eventually I thought, 'Yes, this is enough to build a relationship on. I do love him.' I had this awareness that God would help me to be married *specifically* to Andrew. Because I don't need to be attracted to every man in the world in order to be attracted to the one man in the world I'm married to. We've been married ten and a half years."

Rachel says this doesn't mean that she's been "made straight". When she experiences attraction today, it is still to women, and "early in my Christian life it was a real struggle. Now, ten years later, the temptation is still there, but the sin does seem less and less enticing. And in many ways the fight to stay faithful is the same as in any marriage. I don't want to pretend that my path is necessarily normal for every gay person who becomes a Christian. There are many, including friends of mine, who will remain single for their whole lives, and many who may find the long-term experience of same-sex attraction more daunting. Either way, I believe that what God has in store for Christians beyond death—indeed, even all that he gives us in this life—will make anything we give up in this life look small. Even though it might not feel small right now—one day, it will look tiny."

"Some days just getting out of bed was a miracle"

Kateryna's story

When Kateryna opens the door, a huge, energetic husky dog bounds to the door with her. Kate seems slightly flustered. It's hot, and she's just got back from cycling home with her two sons after school. The boys are sitting at the kitchen table, playing games on a cracked smartphone as Kate fixes a drink. "How long have you lived here?" I ask, making polite small talk. "Oh, we're just staying here for a while…" she says vaguely.

It's when she starts talking about Sky, the husky, that Kate really becomes animated. "I couldn't afford him," she admits. "But I saw this picture of Sky absolutely accidentally on the internet as I was looking at other things. There was no way I could afford him. I'd separated from my sons' father, but we were on good terms that week, so I asked him for the money for a dog for the boys, and he gave it to me. I brought the puppy to the flat and I realised what a huge task I had on my hands. I didn't know what I was doing. The first day I left him on his own in the flat, and I came home and he'd scratched all the furniture and everything." Kate picked a phone number from a list of dog-sitters in the local pet shop. It turned out she and the dog-sitter had mutual friends, and the dog-sitter has since become a good friend too. In fact, it's her house that we're sitting in now—Kate and the boys (and Sky) are renting a room for a while until they find something more permanent. "It's amazing how I rang just the right one." The last four years since she became a Christian have been chaotic, she says, but full of mini-miracles like this. "I think I've stopped being surprised."

Kateryna speaks with a slight accent that betrays the fact that English is not her first language. She grew up in Ukraine, and speaks fondly of summers spent in the countryside with her grandparents, her artistic mother, her friends at school. Later she studied in Poland, and then moved to the UK with her boyfriend. They built up a successful business, had their sons, and bought a house.

On the surface things looked good, but inside Kate felt far from satisfied: "I had everything a girl can dream of, but almost never felt happy. I never had enough, I was constantly worrying, scared of lots of different things. I felt lonely and worthless, stressed and depressed—like I was existing without real purpose. I felt that something had to change."

The opportunity to change something came in the form of a short text from a new friend, Lizby. "Lizby was a mum that I met when my kids were starting school. She knew we were new and was very helpful, and we became friends quite quickly. She has four boys and one of them was in my son's class, so we would meet at kids' birthday parties and things like that. At the end of the year she told me that her boys would be going to a different school next term, so she wouldn't be around. Then one evening that summer I received a very short text message from her just saying, 'Would you like to come to church with us on Sunday?' I wanted to keep in contact with her, so I said yes."

Kate was surprised to discover that Lizby's church met in the school hall. That alone made it very different from the handful of times she had been to church as a child. "I always believed

"I received a text from a friend saying, 'Would you like to come to church with us on Sunday?'"

God existed, but he seemed so far away. I remember church in Ukraine being kind of boring and scary for children—you get all these sad pictures on the wall and candles burning. I was surprised when I came to Lizby's church for the first time. It was weird, yet I loved the whole thing: the people, the atmosphere, the music. And I was so impressed because they prayed for Ukraine in the service. There was something going on there in the news, and I never would have guessed in a million years that somewhere here in the UK people would be praying for the situation in Ukraine."

She continued going along to church for the next few weeks. And then, later that summer, a well-known actor who had struggled with mental-health problems committed suicide: "At church the following Sunday, the preacher kept saying that if you felt depressed like that, you shouldn't keep it to yourself;

you need to talk to somebody. I knew that was what I needed to do. I hadn't really told anyone I had this sense of depression. We seemed like a perfect family. So I told Lizby that, actually, I wasn't fine and needed to talk. She asked if she could meet up to pray with me. As I told her about my life and heard her pray for me, I realised that I needed this God thing too." Lizby's God didn't seem like the faraway God that Kate had grown up with.

The pair started reading the Bible together, using the *Christianity Explored* series. "I was fascinated. I wanted to know more and more, and kept asking questions. I had heard of Jesus, but not like this. For the first time I saw that he's here and he's alive, and you can invite him to be in your life when you accept him as your Lord. You can talk to him anytime, anywhere. So at the end of the course Lizby said to me, 'Are you ready to accept Jesus into your life? Do you believe that he died for you?' And I said, 'Yes'. It was just the two of us in the room, and I said a prayer thanking Jesus for dying for me, and asking him to forgive me and be in charge of my life. And then Lizby said, 'That's it—you've become a Christian'." Kateryna almost laughs at the simplicity of it. So simple, yet so life-changing.

"But it didn't fix anything straight away," she adds. "It all went downhill." This, it turns out, is, if anything, an understatement. Her partner's drinking habit turned into alcoholism: "I stayed with him for about two years, trying to help him with his drinking. But he wouldn't stop. I tried to, you know, tell him about Jesus. And he came to church with me sometimes. People there knew about his drinking and tried to help him too, and invited him to things. But in the end social services said I had to choose between him and the boys. So we split up." Since then, it's been the three of them trying to get by.

That was when the church became a lifeline. The couple's house went on the market, but in the months when Kate was waiting for the sale to go through, the family were homeless, staying with various friends from church for a few months at a time. They got a more permanent flat for a while (and bought the dog), but now they're staying with a friend again. Because Kate's visa was linked to her partner's passport, their break-up means that she's lost her right to stay in the country. She's submitted her paperwork and her visa could come through any day—or her application could be rejected and they'll be forced to return to Ukraine. For now, though, she can only wait and see.

One friend of Kate's described her like this: "She just keeps going, no matter what's thrown at her. She's incredible."

But Kate is clear about what it is that enables her to keep going: "I've managed two years as a single parent of two, homeless, broke and not knowing if I can stay in the country my boys call home… but I've never felt shaken. Because not for a second has God left my side. He has made me stronger,

"Not for a second has God left my side."

kinder, wiser, happier, calmer. I know that my heavenly Father knows me, loves me, cares for me, and always and in everything is there for me. And that's changed the way I think about myself and my life. I could talk for hours about big and little miracles that God has done for me." She talks about the Christian friends God has given her to be her family in a foreign country; places to stay when they needed it; money that turned up at just the right time, and in just the right amount. "Sometimes just getting out of bed was a miracle," she says. "I would have these horrible mornings when I felt so low I just didn't want to wake up, and I'd pray and then somehow had the best day."

Kateryna's sons, aged eight and ten, have the same tanned skin and blond hair as their mother. At the end of our time together she calls them down from upstairs to say goodbye.

When I ask them what their mum is great at, there's a pause, and then they answer with comedic timing at exactly the same moment: "Cooking," says one; "cleaning," says the other. Kate laughs, bending over with her hands on her knees. She's already told me that she loves cleaning. In fact, it's how she's been making a living since she lost the business she owned with her ex-partner; she cleans houses between school pick-ups, mainly for friends of friends and people at church.

Her love of cleaning and tidying makes sense on one level— she is, by her own admission, the type of person who loves to be in control. Or at least, she used to be. That's why, she says, one of the incidents in the Bible that she kept reading again and again when she was exploring Christianity was this one from Mark's Gospel:

> *That day when evening came, [Jesus] said to his disciples, "Let us go over to the other side [of the lake]." Leaving the crowd behind, they took him along, just as he was, in the boat. There were also other boats with him. A furious squall came up, and the waves broke over the boat, so that it was nearly swamped. Jesus was in the stern, sleeping on a cushion. The disciples woke him and said to him, "Teacher, don't you care if we drown?"*

He got up, rebuked the wind and said to the waves, "Quiet! Be still!" Then the wind died down and it was completely calm.

He said to his disciples, "Why are you so afraid? Do you still have no faith?"

They were terrified and asked each other, "Who is this? Even the wind and the waves obey him!" (Mark 4:35-41)

Kate explains why this passage appealed to her: "For me, that would be the hardest thing, to stay calm in the middle of a storm. I would have been panicking like the disciples. But Jesus says there's no need to be afraid when he's in the boat, because he's in control. The more I read that story, the easier it became to stay calm in the storms of life. My friends sometimes ask me how I stay really happy when there have been horrible things going on. But it's because I know that God is in control. That was one of my favourite parts of becoming a Christian—giving up control. Before, I had to be in charge of everything and everyone. But now I can give up control. It's not like I don't care anymore… but I don't try to control things in the same way.

"When the boys' father was drinking, I tried to stop him from drinking the wrong way. Then I prayed that I would be able to give up on trying to control him and give his life into God's hands. That really changed my attitude to him and made dealing with him easier: just remembering that God is in control—so I don't have to be."

And it's that knowledge that, she says, is keeping her going now while they're in legal limbo. She and the boys have no idea where they'll be living in six months' time. But she's able to think of the future with an extraordinary calmness. On the prospect of having to go back to Ukraine, she says, "The boys were born here and they like it. And for most of my adult life I haven't been in Ukraine, either. It's not the easiest country at the moment, economically... but I think it's not the end of the world if I have to go back. I don't mind.

"It would be nice if I could stay. But I know that God is in control, and that's what matters."

Find your more

By Rico Tice

There's one more part of my life story that I left out in the intro to this book—and it's the most important part of all.

It started with my uncle's death.

I was 15 when I got the news. He was walking along a cliff path, he tried to hop over a fallen tree, and he tripped and fell, and he died. And I realised that day that life was short. I just suddenly had this sense of the fragility of life, and that one day I would die. For the first 16 years of my life, no one in my family or at my school had ever talked to me about death. But here it was.

A little while after that, I was playing tennis with an older guy who went to my school. He knew that my uncle had died, and between sets he said something very strange to me: "Do you want to look at the Bible?" And he showed me three verses from a psalm...

> *The life of mortals is like grass,*
> *   they flourish like a flower of the field;*
> *the wind blows over it and it is gone,*
> *   and its place remembers it no more.*

But from everlasting to everlasting
   the LORD'*s love is with those who fear him.*
                        (Psalm 103:15-17)

And I still remember the words he said: "Look, Rico, God lives for ever, and if you want to live for ever, you want to link up with God".

And I thought, "Well, of course I'd want that!" I had experienced the truth that we are like flowers, who flourish briefly and then are gone. To know that God would love eternally those who "fear" him—those who treat him with the awe and love he deserves as our Maker… that was what I'd been looking for.

It was on that tennis court that things clicked into place. I'd been to a talk given by a Christian maths teacher at my school a little while before that, and he'd told me that Jesus rose from the dead so that he could take us through death (it was one of the few things a maths teacher ever said to me that I actually understood). But it was on that tennis court that I realised that eternity is real, that I would die, and that I needed to ask Jesus to get me through my death into eternity.

In other words, I found for myself the something "more" that the other people whose life stories you've read discovered. And really, I've spent the last 35 years living in the light of that moment. Part of that—after being the first no-show captain in the history of West of England hockey, and after the youthwork in Liverpool, and via becoming a vicar with a driving ban—has been writing and filming and running a series of sessions that take people through the historical biography of Jesus in the Bible called "Mark's Gospel". They look at who Jesus is, why he came, and what he calls us to do in response. It's called *Christianity Explored*, because it… well, explores Christianity.

Christianity is often presented as very complex, or characterised as being very dull and limiting. But in reality, it's fairly straightforward. It's about answering those three questions:

Who is Jesus?

Why did he come?

What does he call us to do?

If you think back to the different people you've met in this book, you'll see that each of them was confronted with those three questions—and each of them, in different ways and at different rates and in different orders, came to believe:

Jesus is God, the King of everything.

Jesus lived on earth in order to die to bring us back into relationship with him, and to rise so that he could rule beyond death and bring us through death.

Jesus calls us to follow him—to trust him as our Ruler in life, and our Rescuer through death.

When, as a teenager, I first came to discover these three answers to those three questions, it wasn't simply a matter of realising that this was the truth—it was a matter of finding that this was good. Not easy (you've read that, in some ways, following Jesus makes life harder, not easier)—but good. I remember feeling such joy at thinking, "I'm friends with the God who made me": a profound relief that life made sense, and that I could think of my own death with a sense of peace. But there were also butterflies, because I knew that a lot of my friends weren't going to understand this, and I was going to lose popularity. I understood that following Jesus would probably mean making some tough decisions.

The eleven people in this book had that same experience. You've read about their sense of joy, fulfilment, forgiveness, freedom, purpose and peace as they began to follow Jesus, mixed with some nervousness and trepidation. But none of them have had a life that's dull or limited as a result.

One thing that strikes me as I read through these stories is that for each of these people, finding Jesus took them somewhat by surprise. Some had been resisting Jesus for years. Others weren't even looking for him. None would have predicted that a chapter in their lives would be titled "Finding Jesus", and that knowing him would come to be the most important relationship in all the remaining chapters.

So here's my encouragement to you. Why not do what each person in this book did? Why not read the Bible, with an open mind, and see what happens? You might like to start with Mark's Gospel, about the life of Jesus. (It's roughly half as long as this book, and only takes about an hour and a half to read through.) Give Jesus the fair hearing that we all want when we're telling our story about who we are. See if the claims he makes about himself have the ring of truth, and whether the offer he makes sounds satisfying. Is he true, and is he good? You might just be surprised.

Maybe, as you read about Jesus, the next chapter of your life—amid the ups and downs, the ordinary days and the difficult days—will include you discovering what I discovered, and what the people in this book discovered as well.

Maybe you, too, will find there's more to life than you thought—because there's more to Jesus than you expected.

WHAT NOW?

Read a Gospel

The best way of understanding the Christian faith is by getting to know Jesus in one of the four historical accounts of his life: Matthew, Mark, Luke or John.

Why not start with Mark? You can read the whole Gospel online: christianityexplored.org/read-mark

Keep exploring

christianityexplored.org helps you to keep exploring Jesus' life and message in your own way, at your own pace. It features:

- *videos giving answers to tough questions, such as "Can you really trust the Bible?" and "How could a loving God send anyone to hell?"*
- *a visual outline explaining what Christianity is all about.*
- *more real-life stories from people who have started to follow Jesus.*

Visit christianityexplored.org

Join a course near you

Christianity Explored is an informal and relaxed series where you can hear more about what Christians believe. You won't be asked to read aloud, pray or sing. You can ask any questions you like, or you can just sit and listen.

Visit christianityexplored.org/findacourse

the good book

COMPANY

Thanks for reading this book. We hope you enjoyed it, and found it helpful.

Most people want to find answers to the big questions of life: Who are we? Why are we here? How should we live? But for many valid reasons we are often unable to find the time or the right space to think positively and carefully about them.

Perhaps you have questions that you need an answer for. Perhaps you have met Christians who have seemed unsympathetic or incomprehensible. Or maybe you are someone who has grown up believing, but need help to make things a little clearer.

At The Good Book Company, we're passionate about producing materials that help people of all ages and stages understand the heart of the Christian message, which is found in the pages of the Bible.

Whoever you are, and wherever you are at when it comes to these big questions, we hope we can help. As a publisher we want to help you look at the good book that is the Bible because we're convinced that as we meet the person who stands at its centre—Jesus Christ—we find the clearest answers to our biggest questions.

Visit our website to discover the range of books, videos and other resources we produce, or visit our partner site www.christianityexplored.org for a clear explanation of who Jesus is and why he came.

Thanks again for reading,

Your friends at The Good Book Company

thegoodbook.com | thegoodbook.co.uk
thegoodbook.com.au | thegoodbook.co.nz | thegoodbook.co.in

WWW.CHRISTIANITYEXPLORED.ORG

Our partner site is a great place to explore the Christian faith, with powerful testimonies and answers to difficult questions.